Twayne's United States Authors Series

EDITOR OF THIS VOLUME

David J. Nordloh
Indiana University, Bloomington

Hjalmar Hjorth Boyesen

TUSAS 350

Hjalmar Hjorth Boyesen

HJALMAR
HJORTH BOYESEN

By ROBERT S. FREDRICKSON

Gettysburg College

TWAYNE PUBLISHERS
A DIVISION OF G. K. HALL & CO., BOSTON

Copyright © 1980 by G. K. Hall & Co.

Published in 1980 by Twayne Publishers,
A Division of G. K. Hall & Co.
All Rights Reserved

Printed on permanent/durable acid-free paper and bound
in the United States of America

First Printing

Frontispiece photo of Hjalmar Hjorth Boyesen courtesy of
Columbia University Library

Library of Congress Cataloging in Publication Data

Fredrickson, Robert S.
Hjalmar Hjorth Boyesen.

(Twayne's United States authors series; TUSAS 350)
Bibliography: pp. 174–80
Includes index.
1. Boyesen, Hjalmar Hjorth, 1848–1895
Criticism and interpretation.
PS1118.F7   813'.4   79-20881
ISBN 0-8057-7290-1

Contents

About the Author

Preface

Chronology

1. A Definition of the Man   17

2. The Romancer   32

3. Between Two Worlds   51

4. The Girl   74

5. The Theorist and The Realist   102

6. Order and Progress   115

7. The Major Phase   128

8. Conclusion   153

   Notes and References   165

   Selected Bibliography   174

   Index   181

About the Author

Robert S. Fredrickson received his B. A. at DePauw University in Indiana in 1961 as a history major, but switched his area of specialization when he attended the University of Minnesota. He received an M.A. from Minnesota in 1964 and afterwards taught English for two years at the University of North Carolina at Charlotte. Following that, he attended the University of North Carolina at Chapel Hill, where he was awarded a Ph.D. in 1970. His area of specialization was American Literature, and he wrote his dissertation, "Hjalmar Hjorth Boyesen, Man of Letters," under the direction of C. Hugh Holman. Since leaving the University of North Carolina in 1969, he has taught at Gettysburg College, where he is an associate professor of English. Besides American Literature, his areas of specialization now include twentieth century fiction since 1940, film aesthetics, and literature and psychology.

Fredrickson's article, "Hjalmar Hjorth Boyesen, Howells Outrealisted," appeared in *The Markham Review*. His article, "Gulley Jimson's Painterly Prose" on Joyce Cary appeared in *The Bucknell Review* in 1979. Much of his writing in recent years has concerned contemporary British and American novelists. He has presented papers in 1977, 1978, and 1979 at the Northeast Modern Language Association Meetings on John Fowles, John Updike, and John Gardner, respectively.

Preface

The reading of the fiction of such a minor literary figure of another era as Hjalmar Hjorth Boyesen is valuable for a number of reasons. To begin with, Boyesen was not regarded as minor by his contemporaries. There are today some writers who receive recognition, perhaps even the National Book Award, who will be little remembered after three-quarters of a century. This is the way literary history works, and only by reading those writers whose limitations preclude immortality does one understand the peculiar relation between a man and his age. Boyesen's works are confusingly Victorian, just as his contemporaries were confused Victorians and just as most people now are confused moderns. He participated not only in the real literary and intellectual advancements of his age, but also in the silliness of his times. He did not have the unerring sense of the universal that Henry James possessed. His mentor and colleague, William Dean Howells, who was like Boyesen in participating in the narrow world of middle class America, had a detachment that is lacking in Boyesen. Boyesen is interesting because he was idealistic in an emotional way, because he shared in the Victorian capacity to invest their emotional surplus, the leftovers from their dry social and family lives, in society's larger dreams. He was idealistic about science, progress, democracy, and America's potential. Paradoxically, he was often idealistic about material advancement and affluence. These myths are not unfamiliar, since they are still prevalent in American popular culture, but Boyesen's combination of them with hard-headed Realism, his close scrutiny of experience which heretofore had been outside the province of literature, makes his work an odd admixture. One should, therefore, not make judgments about such a writer by comparing him with the more universal James or the more objective Howells. Boyesen was his own man doing his peculiar job.

To discover how the chaos of subject matter and tone can contribute to success, one needs to examine Boyesen's novels for what is intrinsic, to approach them in an Aristotelian manner, describing what they are and how they work. Surprisingly, the confusion of Realism and sentimental romance which caused a critic to lambast one of Boyesen's worst novels, *The Light of Her Countenance*, for attempting to be too many things in alternation, contributes to the value of such other works as *Falconberg*, *The Mammon of Unrighteousness*, *The Golden Calf*, and *Social Strugglers*. Although Boyesen was often the compromised artist, making concessions to the Philistine and sentimental nature of his audience, most of the time he wrote as well as he could and with high moral purpose. His curious combination of crass motives and artistic dedication was nevertheless fortuitous, and one occasionally finds with surprise that popular art, because it speaks with naive openness, is significant.

The greatest barrier to appreciation of Boyesen is his sentimentalism, and yet ironically, it is his use of an outmoded Romantic approach which often slips over to sentimentality while handling Realistic material that ultimately establishes him as unique and worthy of our study. Since I am to speak of Boyesen's sentimentality quite often, it is fitting to give here a definition of sentimentality. In general, it is an indulgence in emotion which is disproportionate or incongruous with reality. An author may sentimentally emphasize a particular scene in a novel—the death of little Eva in *Uncle Tom's Cabin*, for example—without regard to the importance of that scene in terms of plot, character, or theme, just because such scenes have tear-evoking appeal. In addition, an author may undermine certain values he purportedly maintains when sentiment obscures his moral vision. Moreover, an author's world view may have certain sentimental inconsistencies in it which indicate that his emotions supplant his logic instead of buttressing it.

Boyesen's most common plot, romantic love leading to a happily ever after conclusion, is a sentimental one. Edmund Wilson describes the pattern in *Patriotic Gore*: "The accepted indispensable axis of the ordinary American novel had come, as we have seen in Cable, to be a love story treated in a certain way; the lovers must eventually marry, but in the meantime they must be kept apart by obstacles."[1] Yet Boyesen often unsentimentally placed newlyweds in unfamiliar worlds which were to be challenging. Thus the romantic love story may work for two purposes simultaneously. While it ensnares a sentimental female audience, once it has this audience secure, it slips in realistic truths about the nature of love and the nature of the institution of marriage in a world where change has undermined tradition and forced difficult adjustments upon individuals. A contrast between problems which are resolved in what was then the conventional manner of fiction and those which are unresolved, ironically emphasizes the uncertainties of life.

Boyesen, like Howells, also used sentimentality as a target for open assault. Both recognized the dangers inherent in overromanticizing life. Matters which earlier could bask in the mystic light of Romantic imagination were brought under the steady daylight of Realism and discovered to be sentimental. In satirizing the hyper-Romantic or the sentimental, the Romantic figure of the artist is quite often their target. Howells and Boyesen both depict selfish Romantic young artists who are unable to recognize or depict the world as it was in late nineteenth century America. Aware of tremendous affective powers that literature has over audiences, they were leery of Dionysian devils who might have a harmful influence.

Boyesen was also critical of sentimental anachronisms such as dueling, although one might suspect that his principal motive in keeping heroes out of duels was to keep them alive to marry heroines. Furthermore, Boyesen did not share in the sentimental myths which abounded about immigration and the glories of innocent America versus the decadence of Europe.

Yet while Boyesen was unsentimental with regard to these themes, he was, as his life testifies, often irrationally attached to Philistine values. His descriptions of the toilettes of society ladies or of the fixtures and furnishings of plutocratic houses indicate that he was strongly drawn to that which he supposedly condemned as vain. While he strove toward greater realism in his subject matter, at heart his technique, his very impulse toward actuality, was romantic. Boyesen had a shallowly convenient optimism on occasion about man's good instincts. In his most Realistic novels, his finest characters are not those who believe in reason, but are romantic children who obey the promptings of their hearts. Boyesen's mixture of such Romanticism with Realistic subject matter is often the source of his success, for it allows him to elevate commonplace men and their experience to the level of significance. Thus his newspapermen, writers, scientists, and social workers become the American equivalents of knights. Boyesen did not want supermen for heroes; a protagonist, he maintained, should be typical. At times, however, his belief in ordinary men and the promptings of the heart caused him to condone indulgence in the Philistinism he supposedly condemned.

It is this inconsistency in Boyesen which separates him most markedly from Howells. In Boyesen one is often almost overwhelmed by the sentimental, whereas in Howells one feels the author is above it. Howells, along with his characters Basil and Isabel March of *A Hazard of New Fortunes*, "liked to play with the romantic from the safe vantage ground of their real practicality, and to divine the poetry of the commonplace."[2] There is no distance between Boyesen and his sentimental material. While he had the Realist's penchant for describing things, for bringing new subject matter to literature, he simultaneously brought to his experience a type of Victorian sentimentality. His visions were those of a Romantic who fell upon bad days, who yearned for a mystic fusion of spirit with the physical, but had to rely on surface emotion rather than deep feeling. In such later novels as *The Light of Her Countenance* (1889) and *Social Strugglers* (1895), he stages powerful recognition scenes for lovers during religious services. The singing in the former and the preaching in the latter seem to sanctify the love of man and woman. As in a Renaissance sonnet cycle, he was attempting to make a real woman almost divine, but as in an English Victorian novel, his attempts were nearly always futile.

This study will be concerned primarily with Boyesen's fiction, concentrating on those works which are significant in terms of his development as a writer. The discussion of his early work is more comprehensive, while perhaps of less depth, than the analysis of his later work, because during his early career the gap between his best and poorest work is not so great as it becomes later. Besides, many inept early stories point toward later development. With his later work, I have concentrated on the novels and have ignored his reversions to outgrown types of fiction. Boyesen's last three novels are what he should be remembered by, and they are so far removed from the children's stories and women's magazine romances that he continued to write throughout his career that it would not be fair to the former to discuss them alongside the latter. Hence in this chronologically organized study, a progression from a sociological and historical approach—which attempts to place Boyesen among phenomena of the past—to a literary critical approach—which attempts to define Boyesen in terms of genre, the modes by which his fiction operates—may be seen. Boyesen, too often only a representative man of his culture, at moments transcended it.

ROBERT S. FREDRICKSON

Gettysburg College

Chronology

1848 Born September 21, Fredriksvaern, Norway.
1868 Receives degree from the Royal Fredriks University.
1869 Emigrates from Norway to America.
1871 Publishes unsigned review of Anderson's *A Poet's Bazaar* in *Atlantic Monthly*.
1872 Publishes first signed piece, "A Norse Stev," in *Atlantic Monthly*.
1873 *Gunnar* serialized in *Atlantic Monthly*.
1873– Spends year studying in Europe in preparation for teach-
1874 ing position at Cornell.
1874 Assumes assistant professorship of European languages at Cornell University. *A Norseman's Pilgrimage* serialized in *Galaxy*; *Gunnar* published.
1875 *A Norseman's Pilgrimage* published.
1876 *Tales from Two Hemispheres*, first collection of stories, published.
1877 Correspondence with George Washington Cable begins.
1878 Marries Lillie Keene.
1879 *Falconberg* and *Goethe and Schiller* published.
1880 Moves to New York.
1881 Takes an instructorship at Columbia College. *Queen Titania* and *Ilka on a Hilltop* published.
1883 *Daughter of the Philistines* published.
1884 *Alpine Roses* (play) produced in New York.
1886 *The Story of Norway* published.
1889 *The Light of Her Countenance* and *Vagabond Tales* published.
1891 *The Mammon of Unrighteousness* and *Norseland Tales* published.
1892 *A Golden Calf* and *Essays on German Literature* published.

1893   Becomes literary critic for *Cosmopolitan*; *Social Strugglers* published.

1894   *A Commentary on the Writing of Henrik Ibsen* and *Literary and Social Silhouettes* published.

1895   *Essays on Scandinavian Literature* published. Dies October 4, New York City, of pneumonia.

CHAPTER 1

A Definition of the Man

I *Ephemeral Fame*

WHEN Hjalmar Hjorth Boyesen died suddenly and unexpectedly in October 1895, at the age of forty-seven, the elite of American letters served as his pallbearers.[1] Boyesen was an ambitious literary man who appeared to have made it. His collected works would fill forty volumes. Many of his novels had been popular, going through several editions, and he had influenced such important literary figures as William Dean Howells and George Washington Cable. He counted among his literary friends and acquaintances such internationally reknowned men as Turgenev, Georg Brandes, and Henrik Ibsen. Certainly Boyesen would have reason for surprise had he been told how quickly he was to be forgotten. Yet in the excitement of the literary generation which followed, Naturalists, like children of immigrants, disavowed their predecessors. Like Howells', Boyesen's writing had little consistency in philosophic base; he had spoken no doctrinaire manifestoes. And the new age, as Howells was to live to see, was one in which manifestoes made waves, one in which the rationale behind art often assumed greater importance than works of art themselves, which were, after all, supposed to be artless. In addition, Boyesen's social Realism, so close to Howells' "smiling aspects of life," probably appeared too tame to a generation of antiestablishment populists and pessimistic Naturalists. Indeed Boyesen's own lifestyle, his struggle for wealth, his marriage to a socialite, and his association with the "genteel tradition" made him anathema to Naturalists.

II *European Sensibility*

To note Boyesen's Victorianism underscores the way in which

Boyesen, despite his desire to be the typical American, was
never a representative American. Not even as an immigrant was
he typical. He came to America because it was the land of
literary opportunity, not because he sought wealth or freedom
which were unavailable to him at home in Norway. In Norway
he would find scarcely ten or twenty thousand who could afford
to be interested in literature, his father had advised, and so
Boyesen left Norway for a larger literary market.[2] In some respects, Boyesen's experience with the nineteenth century world
was more that of a cultured Englishman than of the American
native or immigrant. He left a pastoral world in which he
might have lived in quiet elegance and dignity to come to a
land in which no sanctifying tradition existed. As a European,
an intellectual, and a gentleman, his analysis of the American
situation was more a study of cultural forces (the historical
contest of feudalism and democracy), more theoretical and
more detached (he could not share in populist anger), than
that of American Realists and Naturalists. He was somewhere
between the polite Realism of Thackeray's drawing room and
city Realism.[3] Kazin characterizes the younger men of American
Realism in the 1890s as "not even interested in the *theory* of
naturalism, in the scientific jargon out of Claude Bernard,
Darwin, and Taine with which Zola and his school bedecked
le roman experimental." They were "the young naturalists who
had drawn the iron of American realism out of social discontent
and the rebellion of their generation...."[4] While not developing
a coherent ideology, Boyesen was nonetheless more academic
than these. He was more familiar with European Realistic-
Naturalistic theory, but like a Victorian with a divorced sensibility, he was unable to apply such theories convincingly to the
realities of American experience.

III   *Norwegian Beginnings*

The one fact of Boyesen's life which can tell us most about
him as a man and a literary figure is his emigration from
Norway to the United States in 1869 at the age of twenty.[5]
Boyesen's romantic idea of himself and his practical approach to
his own problems are capsulized in this dramatic action. In

leaving Norway he rebelled against Judge Hjorth, the man who had adopted his mother and in whose home Boyesen had spent the years of his boyhood. Judge Hjorth and his wife took care of Helga Tveten Boyesen and her children, including her first born, Hjalmar, while Hjalmar's father, Captain Sarolf Boyesen, roamed Europe and America between 1854 and 1856. Three years after the wandering father returned, Helga died while her sixth child was still an infant. Hjalmar, and perhaps the other children, went again to live with their step-grandparents, Judge and Mrs. Hjorth, at their estate on the fjord at Systrand, Norway.

Yet even though Hjalmar spent most of his youth with this reputedly conservative magistrate, the spirit of his father continued to influence his life, despite his father's remarriage and rearing of a second family. In numerous Boyesen stories there is a conflict much like that which must have smoldered in his own family. The older generation, whether peasant or aristocrat, resisted the changes which the nineteenth century was bringing to Norway. The extreme of his sort "loved everything that was old, in dress as well as in manners, took no newspaper and regarded railroads and steamboats as the inventions of the devil."[6] Judge Hjorth, although not so extreme, kept a spacious white manor house with a full complement of retainers on his estate beside the fjord. He was definitely a figure of traditional authority, in opposition to social and political change in Norway. In addition, he, like most older Norwegians in Boyesen's stories, was no doubt saddened by the "'America Fever' which took so many of the young away from them forever on boats each spring."[7] His son-in-law, Hjalmar's father, was not, however, at home with old Norway. Because of his belief in Swedenborgianism, Captain Boyesen's position in the military of a country under the Swedish crown and with a state church was insecure.

Captain Boyesen was a mathematics instructor at the Norwegian Naval Academy in Fredriksvaern in southern Norway when his son Hjalmar was born there September 21, 1848. After being transferred to Konigsberg, site of the national munitions and arms works and the royal mint, in 1851, his fortune changed when he and his family joined the Swedenborgian Church of the

New Jerusalem. As Hjalmar's sister explains, "When father refused to subscribe to the State Religion and gave up, thereby, part of his income and also lost his inheritance, the family was obliged to practice 'primitive simplicity.' This condition seemed humiliating to him."[8]

In addition, as Clarence Glasrud points out, Captain Boyesen "was an ardent republican. He was restless and ambitious, impatient with the slow, conservative ways of mid-nineteenth century Norway."[9] As such, to Hjalmar his father was a romantic figure, one who dared live with an uncertain future rather than a comfortable past. Boyesen's father had "faith in democracy, progress and America."[10] In *A Norseman's Pilgrimage* (1875), Boyesen depicts a figure much like him, a man who leaves Norway, goes to America, and romantically dies fighting for the Union at Gettysburg—not, however, without having deposited a trust for his son which he can receive upon his emigration to the United States. Significantly, a trust mitigates the risk involved in emigrating. Boyesen himself also had financial support in his adventure. Furthermore, the call of America to Boyesen, a literary man, was not only romantic. His father had given him practical advice. If Hjalmar were to satisfy his literary ambitions, he needed to work in a major language in a large and growing country.

In essence, Boyesen had two romanticisms tugging at him. In addition to the call of America, there was the idyllic and incredible beauty of the mountains and fjords of Norway, scenes which he nostalgically fed upon when later he lived in unspectacular mid-America. His childhood there, where he lived among heroic Norse legends, where nightly he heard from servants the romantic myths and folklore of Norway, would always remain a lost Eden. Boyesen was heir to Judge Hjorth's estate, and he could have lived a life of agrarian gentility out of Sir Walter Scott. Representing this life is a scene Boyesen recalled from his childhood: "I remember sitting in the prow of my grandfather's cabin boat, rowed by twelve sturdy oarsmen, when we sailed forth in state, twice a year to hold court in the various districts."[11] To give up all this, Boyesen must have felt very strongly the romantic pull of America and of the unknown.

IV   *Emigration to America*

After completing his education at a gymnasium in Christiania and then at the Royal Frederiks University, where he took his degree in 1868, Boyesen, along with his brother, Ingolf, went the following year to America. As a concession to his grandfather, the emigration was to be temporary; he was to return in one year. In fact, he returned to Norway only years later and then as an American visitor.

Boyesen was trained by his father to be in sympathy with American institutions, and years after his immigration he said, "I, therefore, found myself more at home here, when I arrived, than in the country of my birth."[12] Nevertheless, we have evidence that the first years in America were difficult. After a tour of the United States, including New England, the South, and midwestern areas where many German and Scandinavian immigrants lived—people whose conditions Boyesen was interested in observing—the Boyesen brothers settled in Urbana, Ohio, which as a center of Swedenborgianism had a subcollegiate institution, Urbana University. Boyesen was contented neither with Urbana nor with Swedenborgianism.[13] Thus it is not surprising that he left in less than a year to work on a Dano-Norwegian weekly, *Fremad*, published in Chicago. He worked on this newspaper only a few months, however, finding evidently that the necessity of reading and writing so much in Norwegian was impeding his own acculturation. Although very knowledgeable of English before coming to America, Boyesen had to work hard to make the language his own. He spent his evenings reading Shakespeare, Keats, Shelley, and Wordsworth in order to increase his knowledge of the language. Often his devotion to English classics caused his own conversational English to be ludicrously stilted. He went back to Urbana, Ohio, despite his distaste for its isolation, in order to teach and thereby increase his proficiency in English. But before his return to Ohio in 1870, he spent a summer in Boston taking lessons from the best elocutionist he could find in order to eliminate any trace of foreignness in his speech.

His first year of teaching at Urbana was desolate: "It seemed to me, in spite of the kindness and hospitality of many of its citizens, as if I could never reconcile myself to the steady dreariness of that place. By contrast, Norway, with its cloud-capped mountains and silent fjords, rose out of my memory doubly beautiful in the haze, and I was consumed with a passionate homesickness."[14]

V *Introduction to Howells*

While in Boston the following summer, Boyesen experienced a serendipitous event which started his American career and seems typical of his American literary life. He was signing the visitor's register at the Harvard University Library when the assistant librarian who was watching remarked upon the "Hj's" in his name and asked what kind of name it was. When Boyesen explained his name, the assistant librarian told him that Professor Francis Child had just been to see him and that he was looking for someone to translate Norwegian dialect ballads. Boyesen was not only ready to translate these with ease, but he just happened to have with him a manuscript of *Gunnar,* a romantic idyll of Norway which his homesickness had caused him to write. Professor Child invited young Boyesen to his home for dinner later that week, a dinner which Howells also attended. After dinner Boyesen read aloud from *Gunnar* to a very appreciative audience, which asked for more: "Howells became greatly interested; begged me to spend a couple of days at his home as his guest and read the rest of the tale. This invitation was accepted, and likewise the MS. It was this incident which had the most decisive influence upon my life, as it was probably the cause of my remaining in this country. I then became acquainted with Mr. Longfellow, Mr. Lowell, Henry James, Jr. and others."[15]

Howells recalls this meeting favorably. "Boyesen walked home with me and for a fortnight later I think we parted only to dream of the literature which we poured out to each other in every waking moment." Boyesen's stories about Bjørnson and the Norse literary movement filled Howells "with the wonder and delight of that noble revolt against convention, that brave return to nature and the springs of poetry in the heart and the speech of the common people."[16]

VI *Early Publications*

Boyesen gives Howells credit for Americanizing him. The concrete effect of that Americanization was the appearance of articles, stories, and poems by Boyesen in print. Significantly, the first printed material appeared in Howells' *Atlantic Monthly*. An unsigned review of Hans Christian Anderson's *A Poet's Bazaar* was published in the *Atlantic* in October 1871. In February 1872, Boyesen's name first appeared on a published piece when Howells printed a poem, "A Norse Stev," out of the manuscript for *Gunnar*. *Gunnar* itself was serialized beginning in July 1873.

Despite or perhaps because of Boyesen's unhappiness with the small, harsh, cramped atmosphere of Ohio, an unhappiness increased by his knowledge of a more urbane world in Boston and Cambridge, his literary output increased rapidly.[17] He published a story and a poem in the *Galaxy* in 1873 and a poem in *Lippincott's* the same year, and he began his scholarly publishing in the *North American Review* with articles on Kristofer Janson and Bjornstjerne Bjørnson. His loneliness contributed to his accomplishments, for he wrote in the spirit of the melancholic alienated romantic: "Half the night I sat in my dreary room in the college hall and wrote with a delight which took no account of the hours. A sort of joyous restlessness possessed me, and I begrudged the time I had to spend in the class room drumming Latin and Greek grammar into the heads of stupid boys."[18]

With Howells' encouragement Boyesen held on, and in the spring of 1873 he received an offer from Cornell University to become assistant professor of Northern European languages. Boyesen eagerly accepted the position, and immediately departed for a year's leave in Europe to prepare himself for his new responsibilities. In this year Boyesen visited his homeland and spent some time studying Germanic philology (although not as long as he led his employers in Ithaca, New York, to believe) at the University of Leipzig.

While abroad Boyesen became acquainted with Bjørnson, Hans Christian Anderson, and notably, Turgenev. Howells and Boyesen had read *Smoke* together the year before, and to

Boyesen as well as Howells, it was "an eye opener . . . to the true
art of novel writing."[19] Boyesen's visit with Turgenev, in which
he established a close rapport with the Russian, had a lasting
impact on him. Later in the year Boyesen was to meet Henrik
Ibsen, whose work was subject matter for a book he wrote in
the 1890s, but Ibsen was overshadowed in all Boyesen wrote
at this time by Turgenev. At Cornell, Turgenev's autographed
picture and translations of his works in French and German
were displayed in Boyesen's office. He published "A Visit to
Tourguenieff" in the April 1874 *Galaxy.*

VII *Establishing a Career*

Boyesen's second novel, *A Norseman's Pilgrimage,* which
shows little of Turgenev's influence, began its serialized publication in the *Galaxy* in 1874 also. The *Atlantic* published a story
of his, but most of his work at this time went to *Scribner's
Monthly.* If Howells was rejecting Boyesen's work, Boyesen
evidently did not let it interfere with their friendship. Howells
was defensively apologetic, although candid, in commenting
on material which he did not wish to publish. Boyesen, with
the confidence gained from his friendships with the important
authors of the Howells circle, was able to establish warm
friendships on his own. The *Scribner's* editor, Dr. J. G. Holland,
and associate editor, Richard Watson Gilder, became devoted
friends of Boyesen. At Cornell he developed a close friendship
with Bayard Taylor, after whom Boyesen was later to name
one of his sons.

Boyesen's success during these years is an example of the
importance of knowing the right people in establishing a literary
career. Boyesen was thought of as talented, intelligent, and
energetic, but the most important of his qualities seems to have
been merely his disposition. He evidently had a power of spirit
which made others happy. As Turgenev said, kissing him on both
cheeks when Boyesen left, "You were my David; you played to
me and the evil spirits departed."[20]

Once established, Boyesen began to give sympathy and
encouragement to a new young writer, one whose reputation
would later greatly exceed his own. He first wrote to George

Washington Cable on February 17, 1877. His letters to Cable, extending over several years, tell us more about Boyesen's personality than any other documents remaining from his life. They also provide a good record of events during those years. Cable, a somewhat sickly, genuinely impoverished, melancholic figure of the artist, set into relief the self-confident, exceedingly healthy, and rigorously practical Boyesen. Boyesen's successes of these years, including the serialization of *Falconberg* in *Scribner's* and the subsequent book publication of this, his third novel, were enthusiastically related in response to lugubrious letters from Cable in which he effusively pledged devotion and, in the spirit of romantic *Weltschmerz*, described his own unhappy life. Boyesen bragged of *Falconberg's* success in creating controversy in Norway and of the translations of *Gunnar* and *Tales of Two Hemispheres* (a collection of previously published short stories) into foreign languages. He said confidently that "God intended to make something very fine of both of us"[21] and promised to help fulfill God's intention by providing Cable with connections. He was sympathetic with Cable's perpetual ill-health, wishing he could give away some of his excellent health because he looks "healthy as a bull."[22] In response to Cable's shame-faced admission of ambition as the "Black sheep" in his flock,[23] Boyesen admitted how powerful his own ambition was and justified it: "no man of letters ever accomplished anything without it."[24]

Boyesen's ambition, however, drove him too hard, and after receiving many letters describing the terrible weight of existence Cable carried, Boyesen opened the darker side of his life to his friend. His problems were practical and financial and tell much about his life and art:

I have two younger brothers who came with me to this country . . . . I had to work for them, to educate them. . . . I yearned all the while with heart and soul to devote myself to the one calling I had loved from the time I was old enough to define my aspirations. At the end of another year my brother Ingolf graduated from N. Western Law School and immediately obtained a pretty good position and now at last my younger brother is also able to take care of himself. I then determined to throw overboard all sordid cares and to live only for what I loved. Then, what do you think happened? My father who after my mother's death had married a very young girl and with her got eight small children declared that he could no longer bear the severe climate of Norway. . . . His life was virtually laid in my hand. . . . Of course I had to run into debt, but next month I shall have the satisfaction of paying off the last cent. Thus vanished my long cherished dream of independence and a purely literary life—I have almost to support the whole family. . . . During these last seven years I have worked incessantly, hardly allowing myself time to sleep. My health was superb & I thought I could endure it. I lectured & prepared for the next day's lecture in the forenoon; attended to my private correspondence (which is quite voluminous) & received students in my room in the afternoon & wrote in the evening until about midnight. In this way I have managed to accomplish something. But shortly before Xmas I began to be troubled by sleeplessness which has lasted ever since . . . .[25]

Boyesen's incredibly ambitious schedule was too heavy. His doctors warned him of overwork, and he was ready to give up his professorship in order to devote all of his time to writing, but financial need must have kept him at his Cornell job. He complained of low salary and attempted to find a position at Harvard, but when he learned there was no opening, he resignedly endured his spartan Ithaca.

VIII   *Marriage*

A woman, however, changed his life greatly. He married Lillie (Elizabeth) Keene on June 27, 1878. She was the daughter of wealthy parents who had acquired their fortune in Chicago. When her mother divorced her father, Mrs. Keene, like so many of Boyesen's fictional matriarchs, took her daughter to New York for its great social and cultural advantages. The divorce of Boyesen's in-laws might explain how supporting her in the manner to which she was accustomed fell so heavily on the author. The Boyesens traveled in Europe during their first year of marriage and then, with a new child, set up housekeeping in Ithaca in the autumn of 1879. Boyesen needed the remuneration from teaching more than ever, with his society wife and his new son. Moreover, childbearing had been difficult for Lillie and she became sickly, requiring expensive care.[26]

Ironically, then, Mrs. Boyesen was a major reason for her husband's resigning his position at Cornell. Much as he needed money, his wife needed more the milder climate and the congenially elegant social environment of New York City. Moving to New York in 1880, Boyesen planned to devote himself fully to writing for the first time in his life. He was delighted to have such an opportunity and worked each day from nine to six at his desk. Nevertheless, he found, as Howells warned he would, that a man cannot support himself by writing alone. In 1881 he took up an instructorship at Columbia College in New York City. Promoted in a year to full professor, he stayed in that job until his death.

Boyesen's failure to provide for himself with writing alone is telling. He was able to publish a great deal during his year of writing, but received little remuneration for it. Because Boyesen obviously did not believe in any sort of artist's asceticism, and because to his wife such a life was unthinkable, he had to alter his plans in order to have the financial security of a salaried position. Boyesen once said, "If you cannot live roomily and with an existence somewhat near a stately appearance what is the good of living at all?"[27] Yet his return to teaching was really a retreat to that which he did best. Nothing of Boyesen's most significant work was written during this year, and it might be that the man whose book, *Goethe and Schiller,* was becoming a standard textbook for universities, a man who was universally praised by his students, was a man who had to accept his role as scholar-teacher rather than poet-prophet. Boyesen did not give up the latter role entirely, but during the first half of the 1880s it appears that he had selfconsciously to divide himself between several worlds. As an artist he obviously was more interested than ever in the phenomenon called Realism, as a writer he was more interested than ever in popularity, and as an academic he strove to be an inspiring professor who produced competent scholarship. If he were to succeed, he would have to blend these roles.

During the 1880s Boyesen established a pattern of life which he continued until his death. His busy winters alternated with summers in the country at Stockbridge, Massachusetts, or eventually at his second home at Southampton, Long Island. Two

more sons were born, and Boyesen devoted much time to his
children. But his literary friends did not mix with his home
life. Lillie Boyesen had no desire to carry on social relations
with writers. Thus an association of prominent literary men
called the Authors' Club, which was formed in 1882, meant a
great deal to Boyesen, for he could not meet the literati of
New York in his home. This group included Edward Eggleston,
Edmund Clarence Stedman, Brander Matthers, Richard Watson
Gilder, and others and was purely a social group, although it
did organize a march on Washington in March 1888 in favor of
an international copyright law.

IX *Productive Years*

Boyesen's literary output during the 1880s reflects his conflicting desires for money, prestige, and artistic integrity. His
short stories, which were collected in books, *Ilka on the Hill
Top* (1881), *Queen Titania* (1881)—including the title novelette
and two short stories—and *Vagabond Tales* (1889), are a mixture
of Romantic tripe ("Ilka on the Hill Top" is about two lovers
who yodel to each other) and genuine attempts to imitate
Turgenev. In "A Dangerous Virtue," included in *Queen Titania,*
an immigrant is destroyed when his personal sense of justice
conflicts with an impersonal capitalist society. In addition,
Boyesen wrote a number of books for boys. His production of
fiction during this period was so fast and furious that later
Howells was to say of Boyesen, "He went to live in New York,
a city where money counts for more and goes for less than in
any other city of the world, and he could not resist the temptation to write more and more when he should have written less
and less."[28]

Yet his two novels of the 1880s are significant. *A Daughter of
the Philistines* (1883), because it is his first effort to write a
novel of manners which is Realistic in subject matter and tone,
indicates that even this early Boyesen was able to treat New
York society, marriage problems, Wall Street finance, and family
relationships in an unromanticized way. Although the novel
looks tame in retrospect, Boyesen, perhaps because he was an
alien, felt it was controversial enough to require its being

published anonymously in the No-Name Series. The other novel, *The Light of Her Countenance* (1889), is for the most part a sentimental romance, but not without some Realistic attributes including, for example, a political campaign and a satirical treatment of an American feminist. The mixture of realism and romance almost succeeds artistically, but more important to Boyesen at the time, it was a great success commercially.

The variety of Boyesen's work is astonishing. Through the 1870s and early 1880s he wrote a large number of poems, mostly Romantic, based often either on Norse legends or on his own optimistic ruminations about the advancement of science. The poems are so bad—heavy and prosaic—that it is difficult to read them now. In addition, a play of his, *Alpine Roses,* an adaptation of his lamentable "Ilka on the Hill Top," was produced and ran for a hundred performances in 1884. Boyesen also wrote a history, *The Story of Norway,* which romanticized greatly the early history of Norway and compressed the less romantic nineteenth century into one final chapter.

X Academic and Critical Accomplishment

The area of Boyesen's greatest success during this decade was academics. He was a great teacher and an energetic, if not profound, scholar. He attempted to communicate enthusiasm and cared little if his students learned the habits of scholarship. A student describes his classroom techniques: "If a thought was uncovered in the course of instruction that seemed to him of value, it was held up more clearly to the light ... and finally allowed to shine with all the brightness that he in reality had put into it, and the student who had apparently originated it went away astonished at what seemed to him his own perspicuity and stimulated anew to a still closer study of his subject."[29]

Boyesen was evidently such a rhapsodic lecturer that he was in great demand outside of Columbia College. To meet this demand, in 1886 and 1887 the college sponsored a series of free public lectures which were so popular that often three times the capacity of the auditorium requested tickets to hear them. Boyesen became part of the Chautauqua circuit, traveling as far west as Minneapolis to speak. In 1889 he spoke from America's most prestigious platform, at Lake Chautauqua in New York.

His critical essays during the 1880s were as varied as his imaginative writings. He wrote about contemporary European literature, especially German and Scandinavian fiction; the social aspects of American literature; and problems in immigration and education. During this period he was a staunch advocate of the Realistic and Naturalistic continental writers, and thus his essays, although often journalistic and usually extremely rambling, served to publicize the ideas of important European writers, if not to interpret them. He also wrote a number of essays on heroes in fiction, the Realism of the commonplace, and the regrettably female audience for which American writers had to produce. These essays of the 1880s were brought together, usually without revision, into volumes which appeared in the 1890s, including *Essays on Scandinavian Literature,* *Essays on German Literature,* and *Literary and Social Silhouettes.* Of his essays on immigration and education, most interesting are those concerning immigration, although his ethnocentric Nordic outlook hardly endears him to an age painfully conscious of racism. He wanted to restrict immigration from southern and eastern European countries because such immigrants would not adapt well to American culture. Boyesen's attitude about immigrants already in America was more enlightened. He wrote about Bjørnson and Jansen, both radicals who visited the predominantly Scandinavian midwestern states and encouraged immigrants to rebel against the tyranny of Lutheran church theocracy. Boyesen praised these controversial men for alleviating the stagnation of intellectual and spiritual life in Western communities.

XI   The Major Phase

The important work Boyesen did during the 1880s, however, was composing his two most Realistic, and in some respects Naturalistic, novels. These are *The Mammon of Unrighteousness* (1891) and *A Golden Calf* (1892). (*A Golden Calf* appeared first in *The Chatauquan* in 1890.) Both no doubt represent the culmination of his study of such European artists as Bjørnson, Ibsen, and Turgenev and handle American politics, corruption in business, and marital strife realistically. The neat happy ending is avoided. Moreover, these novels show the environmental factors which mold lives and suggest a Naturalistic view. Boyesen's last novel, *Social Strugglers* (1895), also has these characteristics, although it has sentimental aspects missing from *Mammon* and *Golden Calf*. It is notable that this novel was popular, while the others were not.

In the 1890s, eleven of Boyesen's books were published, including novels, critical works, and children's books. It took more money than ever to maintain his lifestyle. He returned to Norway for the first time in eighteen years in 1891, taking his whole family with him. He kept stables on Long Island and rode regularly in the winter in Central Park. To support his energetic activity, he worked too hard. From 1893 until his death he served as literary critic for the *Cosmopolitan*, enthusiastically praising in reviews Jewett, Eggleston, Twain, Garland, Cable, and many others. But Boyesen's active life was cut short, incredibly to people who believed his health impeccable. On October 2, 1895, he developed pneumonia; on October 4 he was dead, at the age of forty-seven.

Boyesen once said: "all the later books I have written have been so many stepping stones from the pleasant land of romance, in which I was born to the clearer, brighter and more salubrious shores of reality which are my destination."[30] He never reached in his writing the more salubrious shores, and we will never know if it was in his nature to become a more realistic writer.

CHAPTER 2

The Romancer

I Gunnar

BOYESEN'S first novel, *Gunnar*, the idyllic romance of Norway which he read aloud to a very favorably impressed
William Dean Howells, was composed while he lived in the
prosaic landscape of Ohio. Significantly, when Boyesen began to
write, he did not write about the world which surrounded him,
but instead he reached backward into memory and fable to tell
a story about the development of an artist in his homeland of
Norway. Before Boyesen could become a Realist, it seems that
he had to develop first a concept of the artist. *Gunnar* is principally a novel which defines Boyesen's early concept of the
artist, a concept which was basically Romantic in nature, but
which contained both the impulse toward the later Realism and
the always present contradictions.

The hero of this first novel, Gunnar, is a young man of peasant
background who grows up with his father and grandmother in
beautiful rural Norway. As a child he often listens to his grandmother tell fairy stories and romantic love stories out of Norwegian folklore. The legends told to Gunnar in his childhood
become for him the substance of his life. Instead of outgrowing
these beautiful tales as he grows older and is forced to accept
the hard responsibilities of peasant life, Gunnar feeds upon them
more and more. As an adolescent he is employed by a somewhat
wealthier peasant woman to spend the summer at her *saeter*,
a place in the highlands where cattle graze during summer
months. Alone there, he is able to blend his imagination with
reality. In this place he meets the daughter of his employer,
the beautiful Ragnhild Rimul, a young maiden he assumes at
first to be a fairy princess. In the course of this summer,
Ragnhild becomes implanted in him as an image of an ideal

toward which he aspires. He also falls in love with her. After years of separation from her, during which Gunnar proves himself as an artist and then as the bold winner of other contests of skill, he finally wins his maiden, and they go off to live a new life in America.

II *Genre Painting: Romance and Realism*

As a parable about the development of an artist, *Gunnar* centers on ordinary experience, yet in the handling of this experience Boyesen is neither strictly Realistic nor Romantic, but instead a combination of the two. Both Howells, the Realist, and Wordsworth, the Romantic, despite their antithetical designations, had an interest in ordinary experience. Against an Augustan background wherein literature was supposed to handle epic events and nobility, both these literary giants were interested in the commonplace. With Wordsworth, simple objects from nature symbolize a Platonic world of ideal forms. With Howells, while simple objects of nature symbolize nothing, greater detail nevertheless is needed in order to individualize and isolate the object. The Realist reaching toward truth inductively must accurately observe individual cases. The history of literature since the Romantic Age is filled with attempts to blend the Wordsworthian Platonic view and the Howellsian scientific view of ordinary men and experiences. Two primary examples are Pre-Raphaelitism and Symbolism. In both, real men and experience are treated in considerable detail, yet implicit is the assumption that an object by itself has a defining "thisness" which, like Gerard Manley Hopkins' inscape, points outward toward an ontological statement. Boyesen's work also represents an attempted blending of these.

Boyesen's ambivalent attitude toward Romance in *Gunnar* is reflected in his alternation between the Romanticization of ordinary experience and the Realistic depiction of such. It may be that Boyesen, like Hawthorne, saw the world in realistic detail, yet believed there was a mystery in the way elements of experience combined. Hawthorne in describing "Moonlight, in a familiar room" sees "all these details" and yet in "the unusual light they seemed to lose their actual substance, and become

things of intellect."[1] Boyesen found himself in the same shadow-
less and unpicturesque America that Hawthorne did, and thus,
like Hawthorne, he often used settings remote from contemporary America, turning reality into things of the intellect.

Boyesen's *Gunnar* is Hawthornian in its combination of realistic detail and magical Romantic qualities about Norwegian
peasant life. The transformation of detail to a level of Romantic
significance in Boyesen comes through those "accidents of light
and shade" which Coleridge sees transforming a "known and
familiar landscape."[2] Boyesen stressed not the external shape
of things, but the way actuality strikes our inner selves, our
imaginations. Light became an emblem of the way imagination
transforms experience. Yet like Coleridge, Boyesen needed simultaneously a world of fixities and definites. In the face of this
dilemma, he was unlike the Romantic who sees the inner self
as the idealizing mind; instead, he was like an Impressionist,
who sees the inner self as an overloaded receiver of sensuous
data. With this in mind we should regard *Gunnar*, a novel which
is pictorial, sensuous, minute in detail, and which capitalizes
upon Norway's pagan legends and supernatural folklore, as being
like Pre-Raphaelite poetry and painting—that is, a Realism
with an ontology or a Romanticism without idealism.

As such, the most striking attribute of Boyesen's pictorial
method is reminiscent of Hawthorne or James; Boyesen stresses
the way light plays upon a scene. Thus *Gunnar* is pictured in
the mind's eye as a series of scenes rhythmically alternating
between the darkness of winter and the light of summer. Actually
there is a progression in the novel from darkness into light
which parallels the hero's movement from a life in which
imagination displaces actuality to one in which actuality is
blended with imagination. The novel opens with a symbolistic
chapter in which a personified talking and dreaming lake (an
unPre-Raphaelite device) indicates the importance that light is
to play in this narrative. The opening sentence describes a
region where "the sun seldom rises and when it rises seldom
sets."[3] In this region the arrival of spring means the return of
light. Spring awakens yearnings in the lake which throughout
most of the year is in darkness, but with the return of the sun,
hope of escaping its dark dungeon rises with the brook which

runs from the mountains. "The brook is glad; for it knows it will reach the ocean," the goal of the life force (10). The lake, under the tyrannical shadow of a Yokul (i.e., a glacier), had learned earlier from the free birds about the great ocean where "there are no pine trees . . . no firs to darken the light of the sun, no cold and haughty Yokul to freeze waters" (13). Thus the lake dreams of this ocean and of the land beyond, which the swallows describe as one where there is always light and sunshine. Meanwhile a conservative pine, whose father and father's father grew up without seeing the ocean and were just as well off without it, asks in a tone of middle class practicality, "What would be the use of seeing the ocean?" (15). With June, however, the lake gets its wish. The sun melts more of the glacier; the lake bursts through the dam; destroys a mill, a symbol of man's practicality in harnessing nature, floods the plains; and finally reaches the ocean.

Gunnar is a tightly structured novel, with the first chapter serving as a microcosm of the book as a whole. The escape to the ocean of light is reiterated in the rest of the novel by Gunnar's escape from his class position and from a prosaic land where his imagination is opposed and considered dangerous. The plot represents a combination of the artistic novel of development and the Horatio Alger story of success. Gunnar as a peasant must work like Hardy's Jude to overcome the limitations of working class life in order to achieve the elite position prerequisite to being an artist. Such an escape is culminated in "The Ocean," the last chapter of the novel. But just as the lake had glimmerings of the light which it sought, Gunnar has early glimpses of a world of light which prompt him to seek a place where this light shines forever. Interestingly, it is his own peasant roots which provide him with the sense of life and vitality which push him toward becoming an artist. As an artist he needs the richness of his common background— the folklore of the peasantry—yet neither he nor his peasant brothers are satisfied with peasantry. To the modern peasant, all life aims at becoming middle class, at using one's practical skill in order to become a property owner. Gunnar himself was critical of his old-fashioned father, who was not progressive enough to do this. Gunnar, however, aims a step beyond. In his rise in status he eschews practicality—the means by which one holds a middle class position—and instead leaps over the middle class to become an artist, an aristocratic profession. At the end of the novel, he and the heroine are at sea and the sun is rising over land and ocean.

Turgenev complained that Boyesen's first chapter was a little too allegorical for his taste.[4] The use of light, however, is not simply allegory, for light does not serve as a sign of a single meaning outside of the narrative. Through the use of light Boyesen depicts the world as it is perceived; reality glimmers in an ephemeral and elusive way. The flashes of light create in man an insatiable longing for experience. Light is the force which draws Gunnar toward his life as an artist.

As a child Gunnar had developed the imaginary world in which he would later find fulfillment out of the tales his grandmother Gunhild had told him. He climbed over the smoky beams which crossed above the one room cottage where he, his father, and grandmother lived, up to the *Hemsedal*, the bed where strangers sleep. Here "in the winter, as soon as the short daylight faded, he would spend hours ... and to his grandmother's inquiry about what he was doing there, he would answer that he was looking at the dark." (28). Gunnar's dark was peopled with the Hulder, a spirit of the forest, Necken, a spirit of the water, a three-headed troll, and a fairy princess, all from Grandmother Gunhild's stories. Although Gunhild was superstitious and felt herself surrounded by unseen creatures which she dare not offend, Gunnar's imagination frightened her. For Gunhild, a primitive, the world, while filled with fairies and elves, was not mysterious. Unseen creatures provided practical explanations for experience which she could not understand with her simplistic views of cause and effect. When Gunnar told her of a dream in which she was the princess and his father was the three-headed troll which he slew to save her, she resolved never to tell him more stories. Here the stories which are objective fact to her become subjective fact to Gunnar, material which his own imagination can work with and transform. While the stories serve merely to explain physical relations to Gunhild, to Gunnar they are dramatizations of his own spirit. Thus this Oedipal dream places Gunnar, a Promethean son, in opposition to Thor, the father who represented practicality, lack of imagination, and acquiescence to the lower class role of a houseman (a peasant who does not own land and owes allegiance to a landlord). Gunnar did not understand his dream, but his personal elaboration of a myth is a consequence of an individualism which must express itself, first in a symbolic overthrow of the father and ultimately in a declaration of independence from his society and the role designated for him by it. It is his first move out from staring at the dark into the light.

One of Gunhild's longest stories from the past when the "sun shone on many fair maidens" (54) also capsulizes themes of the work, especially that of light. Gunhild in the darkness of her old age recalls an earlier lighter world, which now, like Eden, has been lost. In this lost world, there was a maiden, Margit of Elgerford, and "when she was present all others faded, like a cluster of pines when a white birch sprouts in the midst of them" (54–55). The maiden, a *gardsman's* (i.e., landowner's) daughter, loved Saemund, a houseman's son, but he was unaware of it. While he had not the temerity to approach her, he loved her as much as she did him. She misunderstood his absence from her, however, and began to pine away and fade. At the conclusion of the story, she goes to the stream where Necken, the spirit of water, resides, and pleads desperately for help. Miraculously or fortuitously, Necken need not answer, for Saemund is visiting the stream at the same time and "as their hearts and their lips met, they heard and they felt the sound of wonderful harmony. It was the tones of Necken's harp. Both had sought and both had found him" (62).

This story serves as a rehearsal of the major plot of the novel. Gunnar, a houseman's son, will be united with Ragnhild, a gardsman's daughter, and their union will be simultaneously miraculous and a real consequence of Gunnar's elevated social position resulting from his winning an art prize. While to Gunhild in old age the story is part of a lost romantic world, to Gunnar in youth the story represents the truth of Romantic vision. When he is older and awakens in actuality and finds "the air, the grass, the rushes" are "alive with numberless voices," he has a sense of deja vu (36, 87). Experience recalls for him the imaginative world stirred to life earlier in Gunhild's folklore.

While Gunnar was still a child, the stories Gunhild told became so real to him that he no longer needed to hear her tell them. Ironically, when his father finds summer work for him to make him become more realistic, the opposite happens. He goes to a *saeter* and finds opportunity to revert further into his childlike world of fancy. Take a boy whose experience is limited, introduce him to something new and different, and it will seem fantastic to him, a reminder of fairy tales and things he has imagined rather than a phenomenon of actuality. The effect of this region of transparent air and brilliance is hallucinogenic. In the highlands Gunnar witnesses in the world of actuality people and objects which he formerly had found only in his imagination. He is transformed, either by something mystical in the highlands with its bright broad expanse, a great contrast to the shadowy home beside the stream in which he grew up, or by something neurological, the sudden overloading of his senses. The senses are so overwhelmed that, as in Keats, it is hard to say whether the experience is psychological or supernatural. For example, "The immense distance dazzled his unwonted eye almost as if he had been gazing at the sun" (76–77). Furthermore, he finds that "the silence seemed to make everything look stronger, to color and intensify it" (82). Finally he hallucinates: "the air grew stronger and stronger; it began to float and move before his eyes, until at last an infinite number of small colorless disks came slowly swimming past him, and filled the space far and near" (82).

Gunnar interprets these experiences as signs that "Necken, the Hulder, and all that was fair to his childish fancy had suddenly become living realities" (102). He begins to look for these creatures, "searching through the dark and half hidden copse in the hope of catching a glimpse of some airy sprite" (102). The darkness of the copse and the "shadows which had been coming and passing—shadows such as summer clouds throw on the forest when the sun is bright," accentuate the ephemeral quality of the light. His visions are like these shadows: "Like these they had vanished, leaving the light clearer for their presence" (102–103).

In this mood of clarity, Gunnar abandons the search for the Hulder because it is no longer necessary. "Into his own mind her image had descended, clear and beautiful as the day" (103). Gunnar feels an irresistible desire to give expression to the powerful thoughts which move within him. Yet when he attempts to draw this ideal Hulder, "fair as she stood before his soul's eye," he creates a sketch of a "mortal maiden" (105), identical to Ragnhild Rimul, the daughter of the land-holding Ingebord Rimul, the lady who had hired Gunnar to go to the *saeter* with her cattle for the summer.

The drawing is not a disappointment to Gunnar, and it earns just praise from others. Like Stephen Dedalus, Gunnar is the artist who "wanted to meet in the real world the unsubstantial image which his soul so constantly beheld."[5] For Dedalus such a union of flesh and spirit is ephemeral. In Gunnar's Romantic world, however, the implication is that such a union on a permanent basis is still possible. Of all Boyesen's attempts at creating a Romantic heroine who is sort of *donna angelicata* and yet simultaneously real, Ragnhild represents his only real success: "Ragnhild herself, fairer than thought or dream could paint her" (155). The realistic trappings with which Boyesen surrounds his other heroines cause them to lose credibility, rather than to increase their reality as in Ragnhild's case.

Ragnhild is both peasant and aristocrat, possessing the simplicity and naive virtuousness of the former and the self-assurance and insouciance of the latter. She is a creature of light, the archetypal blonde heroine, whose face is more radiant, whose hair is lighter than all others, including that of her beautiful, mysterious, and repressed mother. In fact, the mother, Ingebord Rimul, like the other representatives of the parents' generation in the story, is a rigid figure suggesting the mystery of repressed passion—how great a passion we can surmise from the tautness of her self control. She sets into relief the daughter, who represents all of the innocence and the opportunity which the mother apparently has lost. Ingebord had her experience, her romance, in the past, and now her compromised life is anticlimactic.

Ragnhild has something of the femme fatale in her, even as a child, but the role is unconscious, lending verisimilitude rather than contributing to a stylized quality. When Gunnar first meets her, he is struck dumb and can only blurt out, "Are you the Hulder?" (70). Ragnhild is self-possessed enough to laugh at Gunnar's query. But she also is a girl who smiles kindly and who has the imagination to respond to Gunnar's retelling of all Gunhild's stories. Ragnhild is too unselfconscious for her imagination to transform her into an artist. In fact, she does not even know what an artist is. When she learns that Gunnar, after having been away in the city for several years, has won a prize and is considered a promising young "artist," she cannot understand and must go to the minister to ask, "What is an artist?" She knows nothing of the vocational artist, because Boyesen has made her a romantic primitive whose whole life is art. Thus she can create poetry instinctively when she and Gunnar sing an extemporaneous poem, "A Norse Stev," after the ski race. She can dance beautifully and unconsciously with complete abandon.

What Ragnhild represents is the most Pre-Raphaelite quality of the novel, for she belongs in genre painting, and in a sense, most Pre-Raphaelite art is genre art. At one point in the novel, Boyesen describes a scene as being subject matter for genre painting:

All were dressed in the national costume of the valley; the boys in short wool-colored jackets, scarlet silver-buttoned vests, and light tight fitting breeches fastened at the knees with shining silver buckles; while the girls, with their rich blonde hair, their bright scarlet bodices, their snow white linen sleeves and bosoms clasped with large silver brooches, their short black skirts with edges interwoven with green and red stripes, formed with their transitions and combinations of color, the most charming picture that ever delighted a *genre*-painter's eye. (135)

At another point he refers to the capacity genre art has for depicting emotion: "Old Gunhild soon made her appearance, whereupon followed a little scene such as only grandmothers can act, and none but a *genre*-painter can depict" (286). The first scene is genre art because of the great detail and color used to picture native costumes of ordinary Norwegians. In the second, where a peasant grandmother meets her granddaughter-

in-law to be, we see a scene rife with a simple domestic sentiment which genre painters admire. In Pre-Raphaelite genre
art, such subjects as ordinary peasants are used because the
artist sees meaning in the natural rather than in the extraordinary. Toward this end, the Pre-Raphaelite genre painter
might show divinity in common peasant situations—for example,
Millais' *Christ in the House of His Parents,* which shows the
child Jesus being comforted for a painful gash in his palm which
he sustained carpentering. In the painting, peasant characters
are taken seriously, yet rather than their being romanticized,
one finds considerable particularizing detail which reminds
one of the ordinariness of the scene. The floor has scattered
wood shavings; one carpenter continues working through this
minor crisis; a child, who happens to be Saint John, carries water
cautiously, and sheep press at the fold beyond the door. This
domestic scene, however, is symbolic of Christ's entire earthly
life and its cosmic implications.

Ragnhild, because she is ordinary, a land-holding peasant's
daughter who must watch animals and do chores, is like a
Pre-Raphaelite heroine. If she is divine, she is divine as Millais'
Jesus is. She is a creature whose meaning is found in common
experience. She milks cows, sings, weeps, and waits. In that
genre painter's scene with Gunhild, which we must imagine,
for Boyesen seemed not to dare attempt such a picture with
words, we see a simple action. It is an outpouring of emotion
between two women who share an understanding about their
idea of the feminine role in life and their young man in common. Ragnhild is the embodiment of everything the artist
Gunnar had imagined, and as such, his marriage to her at the
end of the novel proves that the artist should not compromise
his artistic vision, but should strive to realize it in life.

Once Gunnar has seen his vision in the light, he still must fight
his foes, the practical brutalities of Norwegian life, in the dark.
Gunnar wins his way by demonstrating that the only way to
overcome the ordinary world is to master it. He must prove
himself the bourgeois individualist before rejecting such. Besides his mastery of the discipline of art, Gunnar shows himself extraordinary by winning ski contests, demonstrating himself the best dancer, fighting courageously, and standing at the

top of his confirmation class. The contests often take place in
the dark, the "skee" race during the long night of winter, the
fight with Lars, his rival suitor for Ragnhild, in the middle of a
spring night. The confrontation with Lars is the darkest point
of the novel for Gunnar because it appears that he has inadvertently killed Lars. Like Boyesen himself, Gunnar as the
artist-hero is a man who masters a Philistine world rather than
rejecting it. Lars, who is the conventionally successful man in
society, well-born but loutish, cannot stand up to the universal
man that Gunnar is. As a consequence of the fight, Gunnar runs
away from the valley to the capital where he stays for three
years and receives his formal training in art. Here Gunnar
competes in another contest, where he is to be judged not by
birth, not by strength, but by his talent, his ability to draw
from his inner vision.

In realizing himself as an artist, Gunnar is like Stephen
Dedalus, facing his opposition in many shapes. His grandmother, who superstitiously fears imagination, and his father,
who believes maturity is resignation to one's class position, both
discourage the boy, telling him that it is dangerous for a
houseman's son to believe that he can become an artist, an
aristocrat's vocation. In fact, the three adults who are characterized in the novel with the most detail—Thor the father,
old Gunhild, and Ingebord Rimul—have all lost the imaginative
sense of life they possessed in their youth. Thor was "the first
dancer and the best fighter in all the valley. People thought him
a wild fellow and the old folks shrugged their shoulders at
his bold tricks and at his absurd ideas of going to sea to visit
foreign countries or of enlisting as a soldier and fighting in
unknown worlds" (22).

When Thor's father was killed, however, trying to fell a tree
which everyone accepted as belonging to the Hulder, Thor
gave up his wanton ways and brought a wife home to his
widowed mother. The episode with the tree seemed proof
to him, as superstitions had demonstrated to Gunhild, that man
endangers himself when he rebels against his fate. The order
of society and of nature appeared to be in the hands of these
unseen creatures. From the time of Thor's father's rebellious
act of attempting to fell the tree, Gunhild was convinced that

"ill luck has ever followed the family, and ever will follow it" (21–22). Gunhild, whose romance in life is over, sees no choice but to accept this fate. Similarly, Ingebord Rimul had a fate to accept. She, however, acquiesced to the pressure of society rather than to that of the unseen world. She married a man she did not love because of the pressures of family and society, forsaking the man she really did love. Just as Gunhild and Thor attempt to pass their sense of resignation to their child, Ingebord attempts to force a similar acquiescence upon her daughter, Ragnhild. Neither Ragnhild nor Gunnar is about to accept a fate dictated by superstition or tradition.

III *Another Artistic Success Story*

In *Gunnar* Boyesen seems optimistic that the artist can find a place in society. What Gunnar has accomplished is best demonstrated by a much later story of an artist who achieves success, a story which is remarkable for its relatively unsentimental Romantic optimism at a time when most of Boyesen's writing was blatantly sentimental. "The Mountain's Face" appeared in the volume *Queen Titania,* published in 1881, long after the Romantic vision found in *Gunnar* appeared lost. Yet in "The Mountain's Face" we have a visionary, artistic boy who sees the shape of a beautiful maiden in the mountain. Unlike Hawthorne's "The Great Stone Face," which apparently inspired this story, the boy here is the only one to see the godlike maiden. His father strikes him down for suggesting the possibility that the mountain resembles a maiden. His minister calls him a dangerous heretic. Only a lovely aristocratic woman, who like Ragnhild appears to be the embodiment of a goddess, sees the mountain maiden and recognizes the boy's genius. Just as Gunnar confuses Ragnhild with the Hulder, the artist boy here confuses the lady with the goddess he sees in the mountain. She adopts the boy for twelve years in order to train him.

After his training under her direction, he becomes a famous artist. When he returns with the glory of fame to the valley, his father and the minister both claim that they have always been able to see the mountain maid. The artist is discouraged, but his

mentor points out: "It is your glory that these men imagine
that they have always seen. The truth is no man's property,
not even his who first sees it."[6] Similarly, Gunnar in achieving
success demonstrates a kind of democratic individualism. He
educates his people both in democracy and in visionary Romanticism. His apotheosized Ragnhild in his picture of the Hulder
enables other men to see the miraculous in life just as the artist
of "The Mountain's Face" trained men to see.

Both *Gunnar* and "The Mountain's Face" are success stories
and as such might appear more American than old world. Such
a conflict between classes which is resolved through marriage
demonstrates Boyesen's Romantic individualism, an individualism wherein the artist's imagination overcomes the realities of
class structure. Yet it is characteristic of Boyesen that instead
of eschewing as a democrat the class system, he works in the
system to reach the top, enjoying the best of both worlds. In
addition, by uniting two souls, the marriage represents the com-
pletion of an imaginative goal. In the manner of Shelley's
epipsyches, marriage makes fulfillment possible. To complete
himself as an artist, Gunnar has to marry Ragnhild, just as he
has to realize materially his vision of the Hulder. The escape
to America at the end of the novel indicates, however, that
Boyesen believes Norway, with its fixities and definites, is
source material for art, but that the artist must remove himself
from its restrictions to another world before he can have real
freedom. Yet it is interesting that this America, the other world
to which Gunnar and Ragnhild are escaping, is unspecified.
We see here in Boyesen a conflict between two Romanticisms
which operated in his life. He needed to move out from the
shadows beside the fjord, to bring those creatures of the dark,
Necken and Hulder, into the light. Yet once he was in the light
himself, especially when it was the stark light of rural Ohio,
he looked back to the imaginative shadows of his youth.

IV *Allegories of the Imagination*

Boyesen's most Romantic early stories can without overreading
be interpreted as allegories of the imagination. These Romantic
stories are set in the old world, yet America figures in many of

them, either in an episode showing emigrants in a new world
or in the possibility of an escape to imaginative freedom which
America represents. The stories in which the old world predominates differ greatly from the stories in which Boyesen
traces the progress of immigrants in this country. The difference
represents a kind of grass is greener phenomenon. In the old
world, America represents democratic individualism, a place
where imagination is allowed to flourish. In America, the immigrant must deal with drab realities, and Norway becomes
a fantastic, legendary place. In both we find Boyesen juxtaposing
Realism, an assessment of an environment and the way an
individual reacts toward it, and Romanticism, a demonstration
of the way in which imagination triumphs over actuality. While
the old world stories are more Romantic and the new world
stories more Realistic, significantly in these stories, the two
modes are never entirely separated.

Most of the stories which are collected in *Tales from Two
Hemispheres* (1877) are concerned with the fulfillment of the
imaginative vision of the hero or heroine. Fulfillment revolves
around the outcome of a love relationship. As in *Gunnar,* there
are impediments to the lovers' reconciliation. For example, in
"Truls, the Nameless," as in *Gunnar,* a class distinction separates
two lovers: "He was born in the houseman's lodge; she in the
great mansion. He did not know who his father was; she was
the daughter of Grun of Skogli. . . . That was the way in which
they began life—he as a child of sin, she as the daughter of a
mighty race."[7] As a true Boyesen peasant, however, Truls' life
itself is art. "He played the violin well" (224), and since he has
suffered, when he plays "he laid his ear close to the instrument
as if he were listening to some living voice hidden there within,"
and "caroled and sang with maddening glee, and still with a
shivering undercurrent of woe" (227–28). She, as a Boyesen
woman of good birth, is of incredible beauty, with lips "redder
than the red rose." Borghild, the girl, represents to Truls an
opportunity to realize in this world that which he had only
imagined. The sight of Borghild "stills the hunger raging in
Truls' soul" (226). She, like Ragnhild, plays the role of the
unattainable woman, the femme fatale, tantalizing Truls as a
child with a vision of her own wedding in which the bride-

groom would be a wealthy, princely fellow, and Truls would serve to steer her boat. This scene is important in establishing the distance between the lovers and in foreshadowing the tragic conclusion of the story.

Borghild later responds to Truls; his magnificent music moves her to forget class differences. She promises herself in marriage to him, but the realities of Norwegian class structure keep the wedding from ever taking place. Recognizing the difficulties, these young lovers also turn toward America. "They planned together their flight to a greater and freer land, where no world-old prejudices frowned upon the union of two kindred souls" (234). In the spring "the American vessels ... give courage to many a sinking spirit, strength to the wearied arm, hope to the hopeless heart" (234). America is the land where imagination is realized.[8]

Yet before they can make their escape, Borghild's family promises her in marriage to Syvert Stein. Borghild's wedding day is like that with which she taunted Truls as a child. Instead of steering the boat, however, Truls plays the violin. His playing, which Boyesen ecstatically describes, reawakens Borghild's love for Truls: "The voice of that music no living tongue can interpret" (236). Syvert, seeing what the music has done to his bride, attacks Truls and inadvertently fires the boat's cannon, which strikes Borghild. Truls takes her and leaps into the water, and they die together, their deaths the consummation of lives which have become works of art.

Other stories do not parallel *Gunnar* as closely in the theme of imagination as fulfilled in love. In both "The Story of an Outcast" and in "Asathor's Vengeance," however, we have love relationships in which the condition of one partner precludes a happy reconciliation.[9] "The Story of an Outcast" begins with a love affair between an exceptionally beautiful young maiden named Brita and a mental defective. As if this were not barrier enough, Boyesen, writing as a Realist, adds a Romeo and Juliet complication. Both Brita and Halvard come from the same class, but Brita's father is very conservative while Halvard's is progressive. Brita's father, as a consequence, hates Halvard's family.

Boyesen described delicately the relationship which develops between these two, implying sexual intimacy without condemning it. Here, however, Boyesen seemed to recognize a danger in such romance. The conflict which Brita faces is like the conflict in Boyesen's own life. For while Brita's promiscuousness at the *saeter* with Halvard and her escape to America represent the total freedom of the imagination, she also feels, as did Boyesen, a sense of loyalty to family and tradition. When her romance leads to the very real consequence of an illegitimate child and her guilt before her father is made known, she is forced to flee to America. Once in America, she looks back longingly to Norway. At the end of the story, her child grown and already a success in America, she returns to Norway to ask forgiveness of her father.

The story is not even as good as "Truls, the Nameless." As the plot summary indicates, it contains enough material for a novel, but Boyesen, as was his wont, wrote short stories which, instead of substituting concentration for expansiveness, were novels in outline form. The story does, however, demonstrate Boyesen's idea of love and freedom, although he switches from a radical view to a conservative one, emphasizing the need to reconcile oneself with family and tradition.

In "Asathor's Vengeance," a much more successful story, a reconciliation of lovers is precluded by the intriguing and seemingly divine madness of the heroine, Aasa. An additional complication is added with the mythological background of the story. Boyesen recounts an ancient Norse legend in which the heroine's own forbears forsook Asathor (Thor) when Saint Olaf brought the news of Christ the White to Norway. The Kvaerk family had lived for generations in fear of Asathor's vengeance, because centuries ago a Lage Ulfson Kvaerk, the ancestor of the present Lage, refused to sacrifice his daughter to this god. Significantly, Boyesen, unafraid of Manicheism, allows for a dualistic universe in which God and other gods battle. Christ the White, symbolized by the church bell, represents the rational, community-centered religious force, while Asathor, symbolized by Aasa's own madness, represents a passionate Dionysian religion. In the summer Aasa roams the forests of the mountainsides responding to a wind and speaking with animals. Often she is missing from her home for days at a stretch. Meanwhile, her family has the concerns of ordinary people; they wish their daughter to be normal and respectable. As their only offspring, they want her to marry and continue the family line.

One man offers an opportunity for reconciling both Christ the White with Asathor and the normal family with its poetically mad daughter. Vigfusson, who suddenly appears in the wilderness as Boyesen likes his heroes to do, is a scholar collecting songs. (Boyesen has a collector of song in *Gunnar* named Rhyme-Ola who differs from Vigfusson in being a beautiful tramp rather than a kind of social scientist, but both the folklorist and the tramp are alike as artists whose talent resides in recognizing art in nature rather than in rearranging nature through fancy.) Vigfusson represents an ideal compromise for Boyesen. His responsible background united with his fascination with folklore make him a blend of practical and romantic, of science and mystery. Since Aasa is another primitive whose life itself is art, he is drawn to her and she to him. He is like her dreams. On their second meeting she has difficulty separating dream from actuality: "You are the man who gathers song. Forgive me, I was not sure but it was all a dream; for I dream so much."[10] Much to the pleasure of Aasa's family, Vigfusson is a stabilizing influence, causing Aasa to remain at home. She no longer seems possessed; she relates better to people. Before she and Vigfusson are united, however, he leaves temporarily, feeling that "he must go out in the world and prove himself worthy of her."[11] His concession to the realities of the world at a time when Aasa needs all of him is tragic. "But Aasa, poor thing, could do nothing by halves; a nature like hers brooks no delay; to her love was life or it was death."[12] Asathor gets his vengeance after centuries of delay. She wanders into the mountains, where she dies, drowned in a stream. Vigfusson returns, but too late.

Boyesen attempted in some of these old world stories to find heroes who would make such unhappy conclusions unnecessary. As Boyesen found in his own life, one needed success in the actual world before one could avoid the dangers involved in being possessed by imagination. Vigfusson perhaps is mistaken in feeling that he needs a fortune to be eligible for Aasa, but Gunnar could never have succeeded with Ragnhild without his national prize. In his quest for heroes who blend the practical with the romantic, Boyesen substituted a scientist for the artist-hero in "A Scientific Vagabond."[13] The nineteenth century scientist was a man who while devoted to actuality and the beauty of progress could simultaneously be the poet of the mysteries of nature. Like Boyesen's primitives and artists, the scientist can also communicate with nature. Strand in "A Scientific Vagabond" establishes a rapport with natural creatures which allows him to talk to them. The story resolves itself in a very conventional way. Like so many Boyesen love stories, there are impediments, this time merely a misunderstanding, which delay the lovers' being joined in marriage. Each knows that the other fulfills his dream, but neither can communicate it to the other. At the end they are joined, however, to live happily ever after. The lovers of the subplot are left still ununited, because the families have decreed that they shall not marry until his education is completed.

"A Scientific Vagabond" represents, perhaps, a step toward Realism in its move away from the mysteriousness of romance. But its facile happy ending remains Romantic in appearance. In fact, instead of there being a merger of flesh and spirit, the union is one of bourgeois sentimentality, popularized romance blended with practicality. Although we are led emotionally to believe that marriage here has the same significance that it has in *Gunnar*, here the emotion has little substance. Yet Boyesen's superficial, sentimental solution perhaps is related to the tragic resolution in stories like "Truls, the Nameless," "Asathor's Vengance," and "The Story of an Outcast." In these stories the real world cannot allow the fulfillment of a Romantic vision. Boyesen was either losing confidence in the synthesizing powers of the imagination which succeeded in *Gunnar*, or he was substituting sentimentalism for imagination.

Boyesen later will treat self-consciously the irreconcilability of Romantic and Realistic viewpoints which corresponds with the gulf which separates the old and new worlds. In "A Good for Nothing" he develops a love plot in which a depraved aristocrat separates from a simple, virtuous, middle class maiden to go to America to prove his moral worthiness of her. As in "The Story of an Outcast," America is an unavoidable alternative. Not only has his lady-lover rejected his suit, but his family has disinherited him as a consequence of a cruel hoax he staged in

sending proposals to six eligible females, all of whom accept him.
In America the hero, as later also the hero of *Falconberg*, proves
his moral worth and establishes himself as a successful writer.
The emphasis in this story is switched, however, making America
the land of practical advancement in opposition to romantic
Norway, where the virtuous heroine waits. The hero is successful
as a writer, a creative profession, in America, whereas in the
stultifying atmosphere of the old world he was dissolute. In
addition, in America the hero finds women who are both intellectually aggressive, in the way of the new world, and insouciant,
in the way of the old. Thus when he goes home, a changed man,
to do his duty to the woman who initiated his reform, she recognizes that because of his great growth in America, she no longer
qualifies to be his spouse. She refuses him again. "And in that
hour he looked fearlessly into the gulf which separates the New
World from the Old. He had hoped to bridge it; but, alas! it
cannot be bridged."[14]

The character of Boyesen's immigrant stories is affected
strongly by the existence of this gulf. In novels and stories which
handle people after they have emigrated to America, Boyesen
is more Realistic, and when he attempts to be Romantic he is
sentimental. No Gunnars can unite flesh and spirit. The tragic
resolution of Truls' and Aasa's stories, in which nothing of the
Romantic ideal is sacrificed, is often replaced by the sentimental
conclusion. It seems that even the realm of Romance and the
realm of Realism are geographical locales separated by this gulf.
Unable to be American without giving up his European roots,
Boyesen needed to find a synthesis of both worlds. And in his
struggle to accomplish this he needed to reconcile Romanticism
and Realism. While Boyesen wished to see the world realistically,
he needed even more some Romantic unifying symbol, such as
that provided by a woman, a mother, a father. In America,
however, as his writing became more sociological, these symbols
became more and more part of a distant inaccessible past. He
did not drop them, but his use of them as symbols did not
"bridge" the gulf he described. Instead, they seemed to be merely
devices of artificial emotion.

CHAPTER 3

Between Two Worlds

WHEN in *Literary Friends and Acquaintance* Howells asses-
ses Boyesen's career, it is interesting that despite Boysen's
reputation as a Realist, only one of the two novels Howells
identifies as Boyesen's best, *The Mammon of Unrighteousness,*
is Realistic.[1] The other, *Gunnar,* Boyesen's first effort, is definitely
a romance. Neither novel fulfills Howells' expectations. Howells
wrote to his Norwegian friend that he wished to see him write
a novel such "as only a man of two hemispheres can write."[2]
The novels which Howells found exemplary, however, were
one hemisphere novels. *Gunnar* is written from the perspective
of the old world, and in it America is but a symbol. *The Mammon
of Unrighteousness* is entirely of the new world and could just
as well have been written by a native American.

The two hemisphere stories and novels which Howells desired
are not as successful artistically as the novels he praised, yet
in a sense their subject matter and approach distinguish Boyesen's uniqueness in American letters as do no other books he
wrote. Boyesen's documentation of the difficulties a man suffers
when he tears himself from the familiar soil of Europe and tries
to take root in a new land is an area of the American experience
too seldom depicted in literature. Boyesen's immediate mastery
of the language of his new homeland allowed him to articulate
this strange experience to the native American audience. Boyesen
justifies what he is doing in his prelude to *Falconberg*: "I have
singled out this one from the countless tragedies which enter
daily through the gate of Castle Garden, like little sub-intrigues
into the grand drama of our national life, not because it is any
more frequent than a hundred others, but because it presents
a fresh field of observation, as far as I know, as yet untrodden
by poet or novelist."[3]

The most poignant aspect of immigration appears to be the

change of attitude required for adjustment to America. The America of *Gunnar* or "Truls, the Nameless," which represents the fulfillment of dreams, becomes another wearisome reality after emigration:

Then the boy came to a land where the eye could wander wide, and the thought could stretch itself far and rush and tumble through the space like the sea-wind. And there was a new sort of wheat there, which grew in the fields, but was as large as small trees. There the boy breathed a long full breath, as if he had never known what it was to breathe before now. And he felt happier than he had ever felt before, and determined to live and to die in this new land to which his longings had borne him. But true it was that he was an odd boy. So when a year had passed, his eye began to weary of the distance and his thought to yearn for something better than roaming.[4]

America was not wholly the paradise of free men which the immigrant had imagined. Here also, Boyesen believed, there were restricting institutions and prejudices, here also poverty and hard work. America may have been free from old world superstitions, but, Boyesen believed, imagination was circumscribed by mundane practicality. America may have been free from feudalistic class distinctions, but capitalism created new inequities.

I *A Norseman's Pilgrimage*

Instead of the synthesis of practicality and imagination that we find in *Gunnar*, in America these contraries, like Realism and Romanticism, idealism and pragmatism, remain irreconcilable. For example, in *A Norseman's Pilgrimage* (1874), Boyesen's hero is not the universal man that Gunnar is. As a European born American, the hero, Olaf Varberg, represents but one side of Gunnar's character. The novel tells the story of this semi-Americanized Norwegian's travels in Europe, where he meets a totally American girl of the Daisy Miller type. The two are reluctant lovers because of their vast cultural differences and because he has a girl back home (in Norway, not America). But in the end they overcome the obstacles to their marriage. The culmination of the love plot, however, is delayed while Boyesen fills in with travel material, a melodramatic episode involving a challenge to duel, and some satirical portraits.

Boyesen, recognizing that his hero is incomplete, treats him
satirically, making him a Byronic figure, so extravagantly Romantic that he is out of touch with the real world. In one
humorous scene, the protagonist follows a fair goddesslike woman
into a church, where he embarrasses himself by inadvertently
sitting on the women's side of the church. Furthermore, this
apparently divine woman he follows turns out to be a rigorous
pragmatist, a woman who possesses "Those very qualities which
he especially disapproves of in Americans—their realistic humor
and their utter irreverence for tradition."[5] This woman, Ruth
Copely, who is the heroine, is similarly incomplete. Thus the
hero and heroine, who are ultimately to be joined in the course
of the novel, are not like Gunnar and Ragnhild, who blend, but
are warring antinomies who need each other for balance: "Had
Olaf possessed her quick sense of humor, or had she been gifted
with his keen sight for the picturesque, they would both have
been more ideal companions, and would perhaps have reaped
greater profit from their German sojourn than they did. As it
was, their views and purposes came into constant collision ..."
(88).

The quality of Pre-Raphaelite genre art, a kind of Norwegian
local color which we find in *Gunnar,* is replaced in *A Norseman's Pilgrimage* by the more documentary tone of Realistic
travel literature. Norway is an imaginative world, complete in
detail, in *Gunnar.* The Germany of *A Norseman's Pilgrimage* is
an object for comparison and contrast with America. Olaf and
Ruth talk constantly about Europe and America, their conversa-
tions providing sociological generalizations which intellectuals
delight in making about foreign countries. Unlike Gunnar, who
can apotheosize a Norwegian peasant girl and somehow represent the spirit of Norway, Olaf alternates between misty romanticization of German legends and a clear perception of German
reality. Traveling in Germany, he dreams of Faust's Margaret,
while realizing that all the German ladies he knows are "insuffer-
ably dull" (9).

In *Gunnar* there is an opposition between art and actuality,
but imagination wins easily in the struggle, for it alters one's
way of seeing. In *A Norseman's Pilgrimage* there is the same
oposition, but here there is no victor, for Boyesen seems suddenly

conscious of the distortion caused by imagination rather than its transformation of what we see. In Boyesen's portrait of the artist, Gunnar is an unconscious artist before he makes a career of being a professional artist. His drawings begin as child's play. Similarly, the hero of "A Mountain's Face" needs someone else to tell him that he is an artist. Boyesen's professional artists are a priori unconscious and natural artists like Ragnhild. In *A Norseman's Pilgrimage*, however, Boyesen is dealing with the self-conscious artist, the ambitious American who is working his way up through the business of art. This type of artist, divorced from semifeudal, nineteenth century Norway, is not the visionary who trains men to see the Hulders and Neckens of the world; he is instead the man who uses ordinary experience as the basis for fantastic romances. While the former is demonstrating the magic of the world, the latter is demonstrating the magic of the artist who gives form, plot, and drama to experience.

Boyesen never asks the reader to worry about Gunnar's egotism; it is concomitant with being an artist. In *A Norseman's Pilgrimage*, the artist's egotism is always a bit ridiculous. A consistent theme throughout the novel, one which I imagine readers are supposed to take seriously, concerns Olaf Varberg's confusion between art and life. Because he is constantly viewing experience as the professional writer rather than as a man, he cannot decide at first whether he really loves the American woman, Ruth Copely, or whether he merely loves the romance of the situation. The following passage describes Varberg's problem:

As a reporter or a newspaper correspondent is apt to look upon the world as a conglomerate of items, so an author is in danger of regarding it as a confused heap of plots, which it is for him to discover, to disentangle, and to arrange into a symmetrical work of art. If he sees joy or suffering, happy or unhappy events, he may merely estimate their literary value, and wonder how they would look in print; and the most dangerous part of it is that, like a dissecting surgeon, he may soon lose his sympathy and fellow feeling for his brethren. He rejoices in a fine burst of despair, keenly relishes a deep and exalted grief, and derives an intense enjoyment from every pure and vigorous expression of emotion which may come his way. (93–94)

Olaf Varberg's emotional reactions throughout the novel are thus discredited, cheapened, for he becomes like the proverbial melancholiac in a bar, the man who pours out a tale of woe and elicits sympathy before one discovers how indispensable his grief is to his own perverse happiness. Again and again, experience is to him "like some magnificent chapter in a book, very beautiful, but absurdly unreal" (216). In a scene where the heroine is identified as a goddess, Olaf has a vision like those of Gunnar: "And she stood tall and calm with the light shawl flung toga-like about her shoulders, while the pallid moonlight, as it were, lifted and etherealized her divine form. Varberg's first impulse was to throw himself at her feet and madly declare his love for her. Then suddenly it struck him that this would make a capital scene in a story, and the heroic spirit immediately departed" (52).

Thus if Olaf Varberg has a dream vision, we cannot accept it in Romantic terms. When in a dream Lady Venus descends from her throne and Olaf sees that she is Ruth, one does not witness a blending of the spirit and the physical; one sees merely that Varberg is employed full time, an on the job artist even when he sleeps. The theme of art and life when detached from its context in the novel is a serious one. What is the artist's relation to experience in a prosaic, pragmatic world? Is the artist objective and scientific or subjective and passion-crazed? Olaf notes the voyeurism of authors with disapproval, preferring the detached, almost scientific, uninvolved artist. Yet he finds himself playing a role in his own fictions: "But fate persisted in turning his tragic plots into farces, and he had no choice but to accept the humiliating position of a farcical hero" (168).

Yet in reading the novel one cannot help seeing the issue of art versus life as a pseudo theme, one superimposed upon the novel perhaps to please the serious critics. The real story is about whom Olaf will marry. In this story Olaf Varberg is to be taken quite seriously. Will he marry the American girl who represents the future or the Norwegian girl who represents the past? Ruth is flashy and glamorous, whereas Thora is simple and pure. Sentimental loyalty to Varberg's grandparents, aggravated by a sense of guilt for his abandoning Norway against their wishes, sways him toward Thora. The reader, who feels compelled to sympathize with a girl who has waited fifteen years for her man, knows, however, that Olaf will ultimately marry his Miss America. Ruth Copely wins the beauty contest outright, proves she is Miss Congeniality when she charms the reluctant grand-father-in-law to be, demonstrates her spontaneous wit before the judge, and wins the talent contest with piano renditions of Schumann and Chopin.

The problem with the love story is its overt sentimentality. Ruth and Olaf have their dramatic moments, which are supposed to make our eyes grow misty. She accepts his invitation to Norway on the top of the cathedral at Strasbourg; she accepts his proposal of marriage on the top of a glacier with the sun glaring and the ice dangerously cracking all around them. These passages, written in ecstatic purple prose, are always followed by unsentimental exchanges of wit, which represent a return to the theme of the relation of life and art, the contrast between a Realistic attitude toward experience and a Romantic one. Ruth jokes about the marriage proposal immediately after it is proffered, making the marriage proposal itself seem artificial rather than real. Yet in these instances, either the wit is lost in the afterglow of the previous sentimental moment, or one is made painfully aware of how sentimental he has been led into being. This is no Joycean sleight of hand. Boyesen is not succeeding at manipulating, but seems instead to lack control of the tone of the work.

Such a mixture of satirical Realism and sentiment need not fail. Thackeray, whom Boyesen admired, demonstrates in *Vanity Fair* that the clever writer can play with the audience through sentimental, affective means. Thackeray, however, keeps his distance from his characters. Boyesen's main character in *A Norseman's Pilgrimage* is so nearly autobiographical that the author's detachment is threatened. Olaf Varberg, like Boyesen, is a Norwegian-born American who migrates against the wishes of grandparents who reared him, who has become a successful author, and who has returned to Europe to study. The question of whom Varberg should marry involves the larger issue of to which world his loyalties belong. Boyesen, who was not established in America yet, was a man without country. The choice for Boyesen and Varberg is vital to their sense of identity.

As a consequence, the most touching and genuinely honest scene in the novel underscores what Boyesen really felt to be important. When Olaf and Ruth announce their engagement to Judge Varberg, the Norwegian grandfather is reluctant to grant approval. He does not want his grandson to marry an American. He relents, however, refusing to cause unhappiness for either, and he and Ruth share a father-daughter goodnight kiss which warmly establishes her as a member of the family. Here, for Olaf Varberg, old world and new come together in the family.

So much else seems dishonest, however, that the novel fails. If Boyesen is to regard Olaf Varberg's apotheosizing of a woman as Romantic extravagance, he cannot approve of his hero's slipping back into the reveries of *Gunnar*. One finds oneself asking constantly, should the hero be taken seriously? In the supposed climactic episode of the novel, beginning with a chapter called "The Catastrophe," the hero is unjustly thrown into prison because of his resemblance to a dangerous Russian fugitive. The sequence and the challenge to a duel preceding it are merely time fillers, episodic bits of plot which advance neither the theme nor the characterization. True, Ruth protests about the duel, but she cannot bring herself to make a rational argument against dueling as might befit her pragmatic American character. She merely worries about her own responsibility in the affair. Less convincing still is Olaf's concern over Ruth's motive for arranging his release from prison. Was it love or merely her sense of duty? This misunderstanding leads to further misunderstanding, a type of game playing in which neither will reveal his hand. These contests of pride are not thematically important; they are merely a sentimental means of delaying the lovers' marriage until the book is of proper novel length. Similarly, the travel material and humorous characterization of Mrs. Elder, Ruth's aunt, a provincial American who believes that Germans ought to speak English and that Norwegians must live in caves, are means of delaying consummation of the love plot. The latter, however, are more Realistic digressions and fit the anti-Romantic tone of much of the novel.

Hence we have confusion. Realistic subject matter interrupts the love story; the love story interferes with the theme which seems most important, the contrast of American and European attitudes; and an artificially imposed theme concerning the relation of art and life is not effectively integrated into the more important American-European theme.

Although technically *A Norseman's Pilgrimage* is not a two hemisphere novel (all of the action takes place in Europe), it demonstrates the problems of such novels. The protagonist lives between two worlds. His old world attitudes conflict with an American point of view. Most definitely, the European in Olaf is Romantic, in a silly anachronistic sense, while the American in Ruth is Realistic in the most sensible way. Yet Boyesen attempts the impossible. While rejecting the sentimental fantasies of the hero, he sticks to the Shelleyesque love story pattern. The marriage of Olaf and Ruth does not have the imaginative significance that the marriage of Gunnar and Ragnhild had. If Boyesen pretends that it does, he is fictionalizing in the same dangerous way that he criticizes Olaf Varberg for doing.

In questing for new subject matter and approaches, Boyesen seems in the spirit of Turgenev, his mentor of this period. His critical attitude toward his hero, his satirical portraits, and his witty dialogues indicate an attempt to be more Realistic. Indeed, Boyesen tries a certain technical sophistication here with regard to point of view that is unusual with him. Sensing perhaps that his hero might seem too autobiographical, Boyesen as narrator avoids descending too deeply into Olaf's consciousness. Instead, the narrator is limited in his omniscience, referring constantly to Olaf's journal as his source of knowledge of the character. Similarly, with Ruth, he pretends to be the researching storyteller who can only convey to us the conclusions he has made on the basis of the primary material he has seen. Both Ruth and Varberg are represented in part by segments of their journals.

Such a precaution on Boyesen's part was wise. Yet Boyesen fails to keep distance and to avoid sentimentality. The problem rests, as it does so often in Boyesen, with his attitude toward the heroine. While sentimentally attempting to make his heroines divine, he simultaneously undercuts all such attempts. What Ruth is supposed to offer is a chance to reconcile the old and the new worlds, an accomplishment which involves forsaking all anachronistic Romantic attitudes. For example, at the conclusion of the novel, when Olaf, who mistakenly thinks that his inherited wealth is part of the Romantic old world which he must forsake, swears to renounce this fortune for the sake of principle, the ever-practical Ruth is there to say, "Think how many things we could buy with it" (295). As this quotation indicates, however, the reconciliation of the romantic and the pragmatic here is hardly a mystical one. Yet Boyesen persists in handling these Realistic compromises in a Romantic way, attributing an almost supernatural significance to a very mundane matter.

The major critical problem with such stories as these is how much the love story is expected to accomplish. Is the love story of vital thematic significance, or is it merely a sop to young female readers? Gunnar and Ragnhild's story works because she is the physical embodiment of his imaginative vision. Ruth and Olaf's story is only partially successful, because their being united in marriage cannot really signify the reconciliation of Realism and Romanticism or that of America and Europe. Although *A Norseman's Pilgrimage* is superficially about the Americanization of Varberg, its European setting and its concentration of all the attributes of American culture in one character allow for too facile a solution to the problem. Marriage will not make possible the easy assimilation of one culture into the other. Boyesen probably recognized that he had not really handled the problem of immigration in *A Norseman's Pilgrimage* and so took up the theme several times again.

II   Falconberg

Boyesen's most successful attempt at a two hemisphere novel was *Falconberg* (1879)—a book which also has a love story, but a love story virtually unconnected with the sociological material of the book. By keeping the love plot secondary, Boyesen writes a story about Americanization which has greater integrity than *A Norseman's Pilgrimage*. The love story helps give the hero back his self-respect when he appears to be a reprobate, but it does not accomplish his assimilation into American culture. Love only helps to buttress a man in the tremendous struggle necessary to adapt to the new world.

The novel tells the story of a Norwegian young man from an upper-class family, Einar Falconberg, who disgraces himself and his family when he forges a check to cover extravagances of his improvident life as a student. His father is unforgiving and forces his emigration to America, where the son adopts the pseudonym Finnson. Finnson settles in a small town in Minnesota, a frontier settlement, and becomes involved with an unsentimental pragmatist named Norderud in the publication of a crusading newspaper. One of the consistent villains in this community is the Reverend Marcus Falconberg, to whom Finnson is an unrecognized nephew. Finnson and Norderud carry on a campaign against the repressive theocracy of the community, which is dominated by this evil, self-serving man. Finally, Falconberg discovers the identity of Finnson and attempts to destroy him through a type of blackmail. When the minister confronts Einar with his knowledge of his identity, he offers to conceal this information if he will resign his editorship and join him in his nefarious schemes. Finnson, however, manages to discredit his adversary and to win the hand of one of the community's finest young women. To accomplish these ends, Finnson must do penance for his wrongdoing in the old country and gain back his self-respect. In addition, he must learn practicality without losing ideals, and he must become a public spokesman for progressive American ways. It takes a public confession to overcome his past and reach his goals. A happily ever after marriage to Helga follows.

Falconberg is a novel which is exciting to read because, in solving his problems, the hero vindicates himself against the hypocrisy of a corrupt church in a Western American community and against the rigidity of an unforgiving father. Boyesen's sympathies are obviously with Einar Finnson Falconberg, whose sin, forgery, is merely a youthful indiscretion and not a reflection of basic evil. His father's revenge, turning the law loose on his son, seems extreme. In fact, the youth's rebelliousness is used as proof of his spirit, a refreshing contrast to the moribund decadence of the state church in which his father is a bishop. Banished by an evil father, he faces an even more evil man in his uncle, the Reverend Falconberg, the meanest villain in all Boyesen's fiction.

Falconberg is Boyesen's first success with a complex novel. Like his short story "A Good for Nothing," it is about a man who is disgraced in Norway and forced to migrate. Yet while "A Good for Nothing" concentrates on the hero's relation to his native land, *Falconberg* is concerned with adjustment in America. In both of these immigrant stories, however, Boyesen tells of an unusually well-educated immigrant whose problems of adaption are those of learning practicality in a country where fancy education and an aristocratic background are little valued. Unlike the majority of nineteenth century immigrants to America who came from the lower and middle classes seeking economic advancement, Boyesen's heroes, like himself, are upper class, educated young men with aristocratic appearance and bearing. Because of their educational advantage, they are qualified to move into more intellectual professions—teaching, music, journalism, or authorship. In another sense, however, they are at a disadvantage, for America values practical skills, and Latin-titled academic honors little impress anyone.

Einar Finnson, however, in many ways represents the ideal immigrant, combining the best qualities of old and new worlds. Boyesen, who often expressed fears that America was getting the worst of Europe through immigration, depicts Einar as a young man refined in European culture and yet intellectually aware of and sympathetic with American institutions. From the time Finnson emigrates to America, he appears to be in most respects a complete man. Like Olaf Varberg, however, he needs to learn something about the nonaristocratic, practical, unromantic American world. Still, Finnson is never ridiculous; the reader's sympathies rest with this Norwegian idealist rather than with the totally Americanized pragmatic Norderud. Both Finnson and the readers are wrong, however, in their first impression of Norderud, Boyesen's spokesman for the American way. What at first seems brusque and prosaic in Norderud is later demonstrated to be part of his strong character and integrity. Finnson must learn that this Western American world is a harsh one, and he who deals with it effectively cannot be a dreamy idealist, but must be a rigorous pragmatist. Instead of alternating between Realism and Romance, Boyesen achieves a sort of integration of the two in his main character. While his hero possesses Romantic appeal, Boyesen becomes sociological in handling the problem of his Americanization, treating this material in Realistic detail.

The conditions of life in midwestern small towns during the nineteenth century, the conflict of cultures between the newly emigrated Norse settlers and the old Anglo-Saxon settlers, the conflict between theocracy and democracy, and the difficulty the cultured European has in finding his role in America are parts of this problem. In being presented with it, the reader is taken inside the homes of Norwegian-Americans to see how they are furnished, he watches the excitement which a contest between prospective church organists creates, he sees something of small town journalism and politics, and he witnesses an attempted tar and feathering, a picnic celebrating Norwegian Independence Day, and an election.

III   Romantic Individuals in Unpicturesque Settings

By this point in Boyesen's career, it appears that he saw his function as an artist on one hand to devote his strength "to the task of brushing away all illusions and painting life as sterile and unpicturesque as it is in its meanest, most commonplace conditions,"[6] while on the other to proclaim a sort of Romantic individualism. Boyesen used barren Realistic landscapes, but when such characters as Einar Finnson Falconberg appear, these landscapes seem bare stages on which a human actor can show himself heroic.

In contrast to Boyesen's ecstatic descriptions of European cities and landscapes, his treatment of American settings often emphasizes the drab and ugly. For example, in A Norseman's Pilgrimage, New York or Boston is referred to as a "rigidly formal, monotonous heap of brick and mortar, pitilessly new, glaringly angular, wide awake, and unrelieved by any suggestion of sentiment, poetry or romance."[7] The small Minnesota town of Hardanger in Falconberg is described as looking "like a large crab or cuttlefish," with "small streets of various length sparsely lined with diminutive houses of nondescript architecture." Yet, these houses "straggled away at their own sweet will and with a truly democratic diversity of purpose."[8] Something then is gained in this democratic diversity of purpose, yet the quaint distinctiveness of ordinary life in Europe is lost. In connection with the American landscape, an intellectual, whom we may presume speaks for the author, makes an interesting reference to Pre-Raphaelitism:

"The barren neutral background of our lives" said the doctor, "in these western communities, like the dead gold ground of a pre-Raphaelite painting, makes our poor unpicturesque selves stand out unrelieved in all their native nakedness. It lends no kindly drapery of inherited history or sentiment to round off our glaring unplastic angularities and gather the uncouth, colorless details of our existence under a charitable semblance of beauty. Now, in the Old World it is very different; there the rich accessories of life, and its deep, warm historical setting, give even to the poorest existence a picturesque or pathetic interest." (166)

In this case the Pre-Raphaelitism being referred to is medieval rather than nineteenth century. The dull gold background of which he speaks serves to dematerialize the figures—in other words, to despecify time and place. In an America in which there is no history, in which the landscapes are undistinguished, in which no Romantic glow colors experience, the individual figure stands out in his "native nakedness." Boyesen justifies his switch from a Romantic view of life in *Gunnar* to a more Realistic one in *Falconberg* because of the absence of the picturesque in America. This "will in some degree account for the absence of Romantic accessories in the present narrative" (18). Yet a sort of Romantic individualism remains, an individualism in which the hero, like Leatherstocking or like a medieval saint, emerges out of an undistinguished landscape.

To be of importance in Europe is a matter of being; in America it is a matter of doing. If Einar is going to find a home to escape from his dilemma of living between two worlds, he must purge himself of guilt by some sort of public confession of his past indiscretions. His personal problem is inextricably tied to a concept of man's place in society. *Falconberg* demonstrates what problems Hester and Dimmesdale of *The Scarlet Letter* would have faced had they chosen to flee together. Man inevitably lives in a community, and honesty on his part is prerequisite to membership in that community.

Einar's success story, in which he is spokesman for the American way, is tied to his story of purgation. As a newspaper editor

he advocates American individualism as opposed to old world
theocracy which the clergy would impose. He champions pub-
licly assimilation into American culture. "'Let us be alive to the
larger needs of the day in which we live, asserting ourselves
fearlessly as Norsemen, still ever remembering that if our lives
are not to be spent in vain, we must first of all be Americans'"
(136).

The conflict between being Norse or being American begins as an identity problem. As such, Finnson's own secret
problem with his past increases his personal difficulty in dealing
with America. Helga expresses what it is like to be countryless:

"You know I am one of those unfortunate creatures who really belong nowhere. I was carried away from Norway before I had fairly
struck root there, but when I was still too old to become thoroughly
domesticated in the new soil into which I was transplanted. I am too
much of an American, I imagine, to be perfectly happy in Norway,
and yet too much of a Norwegian to feel perfectly at home here."
"You have stated very pointedly the great problem of an immigrant's existence," replied Einar with animation. (130–31)

The problem is not just one of abstract ideas, Realism versus
Romanticism; it involves a commitment to a whole way of life.
Whereas Varberg is symbolically without a country, a Childe
Harold in Europe, Einar Finnson lives with the cruel paradox
of appearing to have a home in his adopted America while still
living between two worlds.

The dilemma becomes one of deciding what to keep and what
to reject of the past. Norderud, a taciturn immigrant who gives
Einar his only chance in the new world, is typical: "Norderud,
you are aware, had just now reached that stage in the process of
his Americanization when he began to suspect that his Norse
national habits were perhaps a little bit primitive" (90). Does
one's assimilation into America involve forever forsaking everything which is Norwegian? Once Einar and Helga are married,
living in what formerly was the Raven cottage, they Americanize
their home. Yet they leave some of the old world features.

The parlor, though still glorying in some quaint Norwegian features,
was no longer what it was of old. Some large bay windows projected

on the south and west sides (her oriels as Mrs. Falconberg is fond
of calling them), breaking somewhat the rigid monotony of outline;
an open fireplace had been substituted for the old Norse five storied
monster; the territory on the wall formerly occupied by portraits of
the royal family had, to the great relief of Mrs. Raven's loyal heart,
been invaded by Italian madonnas, chubby-faced angels, and other
unevangelical creatures. (284)

At the conclusion of the novel one sees the hero and heroine at
home in their own world, which is a synthesis of Norway and
America. Similarly, Einar himself is at home with his past.

It is hard to assess the novel's success in dealing with Norwegian immigrant life as it was lived in small midwestern towns.
It is known that Boyesen had only outside knowledge of such
a world. His Minnesota landscapes, while seeming American in
a generalized way, do not seem peculiarly Minnesotan. They
lack specificity, as often do his characterizations. The town of
Hardanger does not have the peasant qualities which one would
expect of a new immigrant community. Boyesen, probably because of his own background, peopled Hardanger with surprisingly sophisticated people for such a frontier settlement. The
Norwegian peasantry is represented in *Falconberg* by caricature
and nothing more. Boyesen does not seem able as Ole Rolvaag
was to give readers the feel of the immense forlornness of the
rural West, nor does he know and respect peasants enough to
individualize them.

Yet even if settings are inaccurate or characterizations un-
representative, Boyesen worked from the authority of his own
experience. The novel is convincingly sincere. Cut off from the
old world, Einar has to live without Romantic idealism, without
the support of family and tradition. In common with all immigrants, Einar experiences great difficulties in creating a new life
for himself. Boyesen is here writing another success story, but
it is no longer the success of the Romantic quest as *Gunnar* is.
Success here is seen in terms of the hero's adaption to American
life. America still performs a sort of mythic function in Boyesen's
fiction, but now that it is specified in its plainness, it no longer
can be an imaginative goal.

IV *Fathers and Sons*

Success in Boyesen's romances was imaginative fulfillment; failure, thwarted fulfillment—for example, the deaths of the hero and heroine at the conclusion of "Truls, the Nameless." In the romances, fulfillment can be measured against an absolute set of values. Success or failure in America is quite different. To begin with, in America loss is simultaneous with gain. In Boyesen's immigrant success stories, reconciliation often takes the place of synthesis. Einar must be reconciled to himself, and he must justify himself to his family. Whereas a marriage carries the burden of meaning in the romance, in the immigrant stories it often is the father-son relationship which is meaningful.

"A Norse Emigrant," Boyesen's first published short story, represents a common pattern. Primary emphasis is given to the father, who mourns with each returning spring the loss of his son to America fever. After years in America, long enough to achieve success, long enough to become an American military officer and hero, the son returns home. His return makes the father happy again. While they are reconciled to each other, there is one fact the father cannot understand—that his son is wedded to his life in America and to the future. When the son leaves again, the father's grief is immoderate. In this story, the point of view creates a sympathy with the father, yet nevertheless the son justifies himself in rational terms to his father.

More often than not it is fathers or grandfathers who must accept the attitudes of their sons, rather than the converse. As in *A Norseman's Pilgrimage*, where Judge Varberg has no choice but to accept his grandson's decision, often parents are forced to recognize the inevitability of the son's position.

Boyesen is bold in championing the American point of view against the attitudes of the old world. In "Under the Glacier," which appeared in *Ilka on the Hill Top*, an American descendant of Norwegians comes back and tells a distant relation, whose daughter he wishes to marry, that a glacier will sweep away the Norsemen's home into the fjord.[9] The American, who is scientific in his way of viewing experience, is opposed to the Norwegian, who is superstitious. Because the Norwegian will not move from his land, the American uses legal means to deprive him of his property and drive him off. In the closing scene, the father and daughter are aboard a ship with the American sailing to the new world. Conveniently, just as they are leaving, the glacier moves, and a thunderous avalanche destroys the home under the glacier. Hence, here the American view is vindicated entirely. Yet in his attempt to justify the new world against the old, Boyesen uses a wildly improbable conclusion which makes the entire story seem sentimental.

That Boyesen was dealing with irreconcilable opposites is a fact which he recognized only seldom. Realistically, "A Norse Emigrant" indicates what is likely to come of a father-son conflict such as this. The father and son are reconciled in terms of love, but inevitably the son will go his own way, and the father will be deserted. In many stories, however, Boyesen pretends that the conflict of generations can be resolved, and that simultaneously the conflict of past and future and of Europe and America will be resolved. In these stories the weight given to emotional moments between parent and child is often disproportionate to what these moments accomplish thematically. An emotional reunion in "The Story of an Outcast," in which the daughter is full of contrition, throws the whole story off balance, creating thematic confusion. A simple romance between the girl and an idiot boy in the highlands is incomprehensible in relation to such a conclusion. Perhaps Boyesen is stressing the importance of children compromising with their parents in the interests of family love, but in this case such a simple moral seems ineffectual in the face of such mysterious passion.

It is easier to understand what Boyesen is doing in later stories. In "A Perilous Incognito," a story included in *Vagabond Tales* (1889), Boyesen is old enough to begin taking the parental point of view in a generation struggle.[10] A son here becomes contrite in a situation which might justify his taking revenge. He returns to Norway to right a wrong suffered at the hands of his father fifteen years earlier when his father had falsely accused him of stealing. Now, after many years of exile during which the son has achieved success in America, he comes to know his father again by observing him incognito. He finds himself incapable of avenging himself against his father. Instead, "He blessed even the wrong and the suffering it had brought, since it had afforded

him so deep a gaze into his father's noble heart."[11] The son goes
back to America, taking his father with him. In the same volume,
"A Child of the Age" shows a similar reconciliation between
father and son.[12] In this story an extremely conservative father
forces a prideful, liberal son into exile. When the remorseful
father finally succeeds in getting his son back, Boyesen has both
sides apologizing. Although the father tearfully recognizes the
injustice of his position, the son's willingness to remain in
Norway and his apology indicate a good deal of sympathy on
Boyesen's part with the conservative father. The son has to apol-
ogize because he has disrupted the family relationship and
caused suffering for his father merely for the sake of ideas.
Boyesen is not entirely out of sympathy with the son's wife, who
believes it sinful to hold any belief which makes one's parents
unhappy.

V *Failure Stories*

In Boyesen's most successful immigrant short stories failure
supplants success. Success stories are always more subject to
sentimentalism; what we would like to believe predominates over
what is true. "The Man Who Lost His Name," the last written
of those stories which appear in *Tales from Two Hemispheres*,
is a failure story.[13] It tells of a gentle, aristocratic young man,
Halfdan Bjerk, whose family wealth was depleted, forcing him
to emigrate to America. This unhappy young man finds America
a cold place where policemen throw foreigners out of parks and
where wealthy women find names like Bjerk too foreign and so
Americanize them to names like Birch. With the lack of skills
seemingly characteristic of good breeding, Bjerk is unable to
find a means of earning a living until he accidentally meets a
Norwegian acquaintance, one whose status was considerably
lower than his in the old country. The acquaintance, who is
now successful, introduces him to his employer, who hires Bjerk
as a piano teacher for his well-bred daughter, a girl who possesses
all the best qualities of an American woman. Although she admires her teacher's great talents, she cannot bring herself to love
a man so un-American. Thus she rejects his suit, and he returns
to Norway in misery, only to find that he cannot live without

her. Before long he comes back to America and freezes to death while keeping a vigil outside her home.

The lugubriously sentimental conclusion suffers from the same impulse that damages *A Norseman's Pilgrimage*. Boyesen tries to accomplish too much through the use of a love plot. Yet in his depiction of the coldness of America to the immigrant or in his handling of the ironic situation where a European aristocrat must accept favors from a former Norwegian peasant who is now the self-made man, Boyesen is Realistic. His picture of a New York socialite is interesting, and he is successful in contrasting the functionless European aristocrat with the energetic new breed of self-made aristocrat in America.

The inability of aristocratic immigrants to function in America is a theme which Boyesen takes up several times again. In his later stories, he is not as sympathetic, however, with the man who cannot adapt. Perhaps this is indicative of his growing Social Darwinism. "A Knight of Danneborg," which appeared in *Ilka on the Hill Top*, has as its major character a dilletantish aristocrat who can talk well on any subject and can appear to agree with any political viewpoint without appearing hypocritical, yet who cannot support himself. In this story, as in Boyesen's later "Liberty's Victim," we have the reverse of the success story.[15] In both, men work themselves down the economic ladder until they die derelicts. "Liberty's Victim," however, indicates Boyesen's growing ideological conservatism, for the protagonist is not debilitated by his aristocratic upbringing alone; he is ruined by his liberal views. The youth desires to work only at jobs in which he fulfills himself and advances the cause of liberty. In effect, it seems that like the grasshopper, he desires freedom from toil. Finding each job he holds ignominious, he leaves only to hold down a worse job. Instead of being the servant of liberty, he appears to be the spoiled child, the victim of a too permissive conscience. "Monk Tellenbach's Exile" is also about an intellectual aristocrat whose fine sensibilities are not sufficient for success in America.[16]

Boyesen not only seemed to change his mind as he aged about the reason for failure among aristocratic immigrants, but his treatment of the peasant immigrants changed also. Significantly, this change in attitude reflects his growing belief in individualism.

In "A Dangerous Virtue," he is sympathetic with the idealistic, simple man who is undone by American institutions. He stresses the hero's strength, implying that even the strong can be beaten in a heartless society: "There was an expression of determination, perhaps obstinacy, in his roughly hewn features, and yet there was something sweet and tender lurking somewhere under the ragged surface, softening the harsh effect of nature's hasty workmanship."[17]

In this story a peasant, Anders Rustad, the youngest child in his family, emigrates to America to prevent the necessity of subdividing the family's land and thereby making the whole family poor. He takes his entire fortune, fifteen hundred dollars, with him to America to establish a new life. Upon arrival he places his money in the Immigrant Savings Bank and Trust Company. At this point Anders has confidence in the benevolence of American institutions. The building "was something solid and tangible; no flimsy ornaments, no whimsical striving for originality in design, everywhere square blocks of stone with an air of stability and grave decorum about them which left no room for doubt as to the civic weight and responsibility of the men who erected them" (200). This tribute to the honesty of utilitarian American architecture is ironic. Compared to the baroque sham of European institutions, the apparent civic-mindedness found here moves Rustad. Yet the bank is not deserving of his trust. The next day the bank is "busted," closed, and the hero's fortune lost. In a spirit of anarchistic individualism, he asks justice of the man who, knowing the bank would fold, took his money. He breaks into the banker's Fifth Avenue mansion during a dinner party celebrating the plutocrat's birthday. The guests have just been discussing the horridness and rebelliousness of the working class who have not "our fine sensibilities" (226). Rustad looks in: "There sat the thief, prosperous and honored, and upon his splendid board were heaped up the toil of a thousand crushed and miserable creatures, the hope and faith and happiness of the hungry, the needy and the oppressed,—all to be devoured in a leisure hour by a company of idle triflers" (228).

He breaks into the house and furiously attacks the banker. In moments he is hustled off to jail by the police. The banker, however, refuses to press charges, and so the hero comes back again, this time murdering the banker. At the end of the story, Rustad is cleared of the murder charge on the grounds of insanity, a plea which he refuses to make. To society as a whole, his sense of justice, revealed in a passionate if not wholly literate speech of his which was read in court, seems mere insanity. When he dies at the end, apparently of a broken spirit, it seems that it is his dangerous virtue, his sense of justice, which has broken him.

Significantly, this is Boyesen's only story of failure in the new world in which the blame is to be placed on society. In all the others it is a weakness in the individual which causes his destruction. Boyesen's allowing his hero to be destroyed because he possesses a tragic virtue represents a fidelity to his material which avoids the easy or the sentimental solution. As in "Truls, the Nameless," nothing of his vision is compromised. Yet here it is a Realistic view of man encountering a hostile world rather than a Romantic view of love in death. In both, however, the truth of conviction is more important than the viewpoint of society.

It is ironic that the same author who wrote such a radical statement as "A Dangerous Virtue" could write years later the story "A Disastrous Partnership," in which a Norwegian peasant who has the same proclivities as Anders Rustad is condemned for remaining a simple peasant and for his tendency to resort to violence to defend his honor.[18] Truls Bergerson remains lower class and old world when his business prospers. His partner, James (formerly Jens) Moe, is praised for adopting bourgeois ways. Moe, a Norse-American who marries an American socialite and who adopts the same lifestyle as the banker in "A Dangerous Virtue," proves himself superior by being adaptable to American culture.

The story includes a magnificent dinner party scene which is worthy of Howells in the mode of Realistic comedies of manners. Yet there is too much didacticism, too much defensive Philistinism, for the work to be convincingly Realistic. The impediment to Realistic writing here is no longer a commitment to Romanticism as such. Instead it appears that Boyesen's sentimentalism undermines the Realistic subject matter.

VI *Emigration Viewed Romantically*

The natural assumption made about a writer like Boyesen, who
wrote a romance for his first novel and later was one of the
strongest advocates of Realism, is that he progressed steadily
from Romance to Realism. His immigrant stories, which are at
least Realistic in subject matter, seem then a stepping stone
along the way. But these stories are in one respect as Romantic
as anything before. Boyesen still sought in his immigrant stories
a kind of cosmic viewpoint. His Romantic synthesis based on love
is lost, but we see already here a sort of Romantic Spencerian-
ism, the Romantic Naturalism of Social Darwinism which sees
evolution optimistically, which stresses the ameliorative qualities
of a heterogeneous civilization in which adaptation contributes
to social good and progress. True, Boyesen felt that too much
heterogeneity was dangerous—no miscegenation and no southern
Europeans, please—but he was more conscious of the decadence
of the old world. Like most Americans, he believed that this
country could avoid making the mistakes of the old world. His
view of America as the garden, a second Eden, is Romantic.
Even the blatant Philistinism of "A Disastrous Partnership" can
be justified in terms of Romanticism. The Americanized Moe
"had assimilated himself to the new world, and plunged into the
rushing current that bore mankind onward."[19] By today's standards Moe seems glaringly Philistine, and the current now seems
hardly a noble force, but such "assimilation" for Boyesen, a man
whose mind was instinctively Romantic, is transcendental. Even
in his darker stories of failure in America, he usually blamed
such misfortune on the hero's failure to be assimilated.

Boyesen provides a good example of Romantic Naturalism in
American literature of this period. This Naturalism is found in
Whitman's "Urge, urge, urge, always the procreant urge."[20] It
is vitalism in which the force of idealism is blended with the
force of a misunderstood body: imagination becomes id. Boyesen,
who like many Victorians did not recognize the force of sex,
could not, once in America, separate the spiritual goal of Jonathan Edwards from the great materialistic goal of Benjamin
Franklin. To many, the Victorian period today represents hypocrisy, the Victorian ideals of purity and progress mere sham. The

confused artist, however, participated in the sham, vainly attempting to make it transcendental. In so doing he often compounded gross sentimentalism with efforts at self-justification. If he could transform Philistinism into something transcendent, he could justify the role of the artist in society. As a consequence of these efforts, much of Boyesen's fiction seems didactic and sentimental. His emotionalism seems a superficial flurry, wasting artistic energies which should have been directed at deeper problems of society. Yet Boyesen sought for a myth, a picture of success, progress, and ideal beauty. And what if he had found it? Then would not those other problems have faded away?

CHAPTER 4

The Girl

THE attention paid to women in novels of the last quarter of the nineteenth century is phenomenal, and it is clear that both the latent physical desires and the spiritual aspirations of American society especially were symbolized by women. Edmund Wilson quotes numerous examples of "the girl" who is "at the center of almost every American novel." " 'The girl' has become the ideal, the touchstone, the democratic princess who may turn up in any household and keep the family in breathless suspense as to whom she is going to marry."[1] The decision which she faced in novel after novel was hardly just a personal matter, but tantamount to deciding the future course of civilization itself. In reviewing Ronald Pearsall's book, *The Worm in the Bud*, Noel Annan says, "In Western Civilization women had never before been put upon such a pedestal of virtue as in Victorian times."[2] In a materialistic age in which men feared the loss of spirit, women represented the possibility that spirituality could be preserved. While in Europe this function was that of the romantic heroine of the viceregal court and the Virgin of Catholic countries, in America these were "replaced by the mother."[3]

American Victorians wandering in their garden which was a new Eden were more obsessed with "the girl" than Europeans were, observed William Wasserstrom, because "the American girl embodied her society."[4] If America in myth represented a new beginning, a prelapsarian world, then the American woman was Eve. Man could turn to her, breathless with desire, hoping that she would not start man on another series of blunders. Instead, this Eve could show man the liberty of a world before the fall, a world in which sex is the linking of man and woman "in happy nuptial League,"[5] in which the love of woman ennobles

74

man and spiritualizes him. In practice, this woman wedded flesh and spirit. But since the ideology was otherworldly and Puritan, the fleshly side was unmentionable; as Wasserstrom observes further, "Rooted in the eighteenth century idea about natural nobility, manliness signified a state of the soul which negated the claims of the body; womanliness resulted when the body was eliminated."[6]

The American man, materialist, pragmatist, and physical conquerer of a wilderness, was not, however, in Boyesen's work negating "the claims of the body." Nor was the American girl—whose freedom from restraint Boyesen symbolizes in his caricature of a feminist, Delia Saunders, who crusades for a looser fitting undergarment called "The Emancipation Waist"—eliminating the body.[7] America had meant a type of physical freedom in all the popular myths. American history revolved around antitheses: Puritanism and deism, mysticism and utilitarianism, Christianity and capitalism. What "the girl" often represented in American letters was the opportunity to reconcile these, to give us reassurance that we after all were still innocent, and at the same time to offer us experience and excitement, the chance to be free of restraint, cavorting in the wilderness.

Boyesen represents both the American and the European side of this obsession with the girl. Like many Europeans, he was objectively fascinated with this new phenomenon, the American girl, a creature most conspicuous while traveling in Europe. This girl, armored in naivete, ignorance, and guilelessness, drew attention wherever she went. To the European she epitomized America. Boyesen called her the personification of the Declaration of Independence.[8] Though she represented what was vulgar about America, she also represented what was charming. Thus Europeans could not maintain disinterest in this kind of girl; her mythic importance became international. For example, the English ambassador to the United States praised her, saying. "No country seems to owe more to its women, nor to owe them so much of what is best in social institutions."[9] According to Wasserstrom, "Finally, she came to symbolize, in the opinion of European visitors to America near the end of the century, the essence of American democracy itself."[10]

I *The Realistic Representative Woman*

Boyesen attempted, as we have already seen in "A Man Who Lost His Name" and *A Norseman's Pilgrimage*, to convey the essence of America in a female character. What he tried was a mixture of a Romanticized ideal woman and a Realistic representative woman. These women did not represent a world in charming miniature, as did the Pre-Raphaelite heroine of *Gunnar*, Ragnhild. Their world was the vast conglomerate America, a world so incomprehensible that only an abstraction or a generalization could represent it. Boyesen as an outsider was quick to generalize on the qualities of American women; he saw them as a type, or at best as types, rather than in individualizing detail. This is characteristic of the newcomer bewildered by the variety of American people and yet struck by the obvious distinctions between these people and Europeans. Further, the influence of Bjørnson and other European writers of a sociological bent may have caused Boyesen to believe that personality is "discovered in milieu and defined by certain qualities of caste: a man does this or that because elder sons are predictable."[11]

It has been noted already what this means in terms of characterization in Boyesen's work. The people of *Gunnar* are houseman, houseman's son, gardsman, gardsman's daughter, grandmother, minister, and other categorically defined people. One has the sense of typicality one finds in children's stories that once upon a time something happened and then they lived happily ever after, a story which takes place in every charming European village. Yet the characterizations in Boyesen's *Gunnar* appear not to be arrived at inductively like scientific generalizations. Boyesen seems to move deductively, the characters having been deduced from an ideal.

That the idealized Romantic heroine reconciles spirit and flesh, time and eternity, Boyesen and others have demonstrated. When Boyesen became a Realist, he seemed to want to demonstrate that a woman realistically defined in terms of the social norm also serves to bring about such nearly mystical reconciliations. Thus this Norwegian-born American was unconsciously contributing to a myth which is basic to America. From the beginning Americans had been confusing spiritual with material matters, so that getting rich or establishing a national bank became sanctified goals. Boyesen joined the confusion enthusiastically, trying to make an ethereal Romantic heroine out of the normal American woman. His basic excuse for doing so is that he was charmed: "When we consider what malodorous things may have been distilled into the fragrance of the rose and the lily, it is scarcely worthwhile to regret a remote grandmother's mendacity which in the granddaughter is evaporating into archness and witchery, lending charm to her speech and a more exquisite flavor to her personality."[12]

It is because of such distillation that Boyesen's handling of heroines is so very interesting. Just as his immigrant stories mix Realism and Romanticism, combining the facts of immigrant life with Romantic myths about evolution and progress, so these stories show American women who somehow, though realistically defined down to details of their costumes and often ironically described, represent the mysterious promise of the new world.

Ironically Boyesen, while directing his intellectual energy toward becoming a Realistic writer, directed his emotional energy toward the creation of a Romantic heroine. Unable to be profoundly psychological, Boyesen could not, like Henry James, find mystery in the myriad possibilities of the human mind. Instead he chose the direction of American popular culture—a culture which revered the Gibson girl. Boyesen seemed to try to make all of the facts which went together in American womanhood into an ideal. Yet as a Realist he felt compelled to enumerate the mundane ingredients which made up the girl he idolized.

The American heroines in most of his early fiction are too much stereotypes for them to succeed in achieving the Romantic reconciliation he seems to desire. Perhaps the "malodorous" elements Boyesen added to Ruth Copely in *A Norseman's Pilgrimage* are more memorable than his attempt at a synthesis. Her irreverence for tradition, her Puritanism, and her aggressiveness are all unpleasant elements to Varberg. Yet a synthesis, like Boyesen's lily or rose, requires in its making antithetical parts, and the disagreeable ingredients which Ruth possesses might contribute to her glory. It was Boyesen's effort to make her purely and simply all-American that caused him to fail here.

When Ruth Copely points out in defensive Puritanic chauvinism
that drunkenness is certainly more common among European
barons than it is among Massachusetts shoemakers, she is merely
an American stereotype.[13] Similarly, the American heroine of
"The Man Who Lost His Name" is stereotypically provincial and
insensitive when she asks the Norwegian Bjerk to sing a song of
his country: "Yes, do sing a Swedish song."[14] Both represent
Boyesen's attempt to write a sort of sociological Realism.

II *Categories of Heroines*

When in critical writing he spoke as a Realist, Boyesen expressed interest in a highly individualized girl. In an article
written one year before his death, he traced the evolution of the
heroine. Neglecting the eighteenth century English novelists entirely, forgetting the psychological intricacy of Richardson, Boyesen is poor as a literary historian. He praises the progress made
toward Realistic heroines which culminates in George Eliot's
Middlemarch. As examples of lamentably unindividualized Romantic heroines, he cites those of Scott and Dickens, although
his discussion of Dickens is weakened by inaccuracy. Boyesen
sees no distinction between the heroine Florence in *Dombey
and Son* and Esther in *Bleak House* and refers to Esther Summerson as Edith Summerson. He remembers Rosamond Vincy and
Dorothea Brooke of *Middlemarch,* however, as highly individualized characters. They stand out because "There is no sort of
pretense that they were transcendent, perfect, supremely adorable."[15] Yet even in his praise of these characterizations, Boyesen
has in mind larger categories to which these heroines belong.
Dorothea's mistake in marriage is one common among girls with
her aspirations. Lydgate's marriage to Rosamond, like many marriages to shallow, pretty girls, ruins his life.[16]

Boyesen's tendency to regard women in terms of categories is
more apparent in his essay "Types of American Women" in
Literary and Social Silhouettes. He begins this essay, however,
with a complaint about the indistinctiveness of women: "Because
the feminine ideal for the average man is an unindividualized or
but faintly individualized creature—a mere personification of
the sex, as it were—the majority of girls pay homage to this un-

worthy ideal by simulating a clinging dependence and a feature-
less blankness of character. They repress their real selves, or
consciously or unconsciously disguise them" (3–4). Boyesen
points out, however, that women who deviate from "the accepted
traditional type of womanhood which is supposed to have the
sanctions of the Bible" become "more revolutionary in speech
and conduct than men similarly inclined" (4). If a woman in
Europe were "not content to be a mere embodiment of her sex,"
she would find herself "tabooed by the best society and made
the target of cheap ridicule." Boyesen notes with qualified
pleasure that "American women have more vivacity, more
character, more freedom of speech and manners than the woman
of England, or Germany" (5).

Yet Boyesen still sees these American women as "types," unindividualized, and his description of the two major categories of
American women is hardly flattering. He describes the Western
woman as

slangy in her speech, careless in her pronunciation and bent upon
"having a good time" without reference to the prohibitions which are
framed for the special purpose of annoying women. I was sometimes
in danger of misinterpreting her conduct, but soon came to the conclusion that there was no harm in her. She ruled her father and her
mother. . . . She had about as much idea of propriety (in the European sense) as a cat has of mathematics. . . . Patriotic she was—
bristling with combativeness if a criticism was made which implied
disrespect of American manners or institutions. She was good-natured,
generous to a fault, and brimming with energy. (7–8)

This is the American woman one encounters in European fiction.
"Ouida has caricatured her in *Moths* and Sardou in *L'Oncle
Sam*," and to Boyesen she is "not a wholly agreeable phenom-
enon" (10).

Another type of American woman is "The Aspiring Woman."
This woman

is not handsome . . . is not conspicuous for taste in dress. She regards
dress and all other things which have no bearing upon her intellectual
development as being of slight consequence. . . . she rebukes you
with a glance of mild reprobation if you indulge in "frivolous talk"

or refer to any physical traits in a member of her sex. There is no
affectation in this; it is rather the result of a long puritanic descent,
and amounts to a second conscience. She knows the flesh only as
something to be mortified, and though she may have abandoned the
scriptural grounds for the mortification, she is, in the midst of her
consciousness of evil, so good as almost to be able to dispense with
the commandments. I have known her skeptical and I have known
her religious; but skepticism sat lightly upon her, like a divestible
garment, and could not conceal her innate goodness. She is frequently
aenemic, and in New England inclines to be flat chested. The vigors
of her physical life usually leave much to be desired; the poverty of
diet in ascetic ancestors has often reduced her vitality, making her
undervalue the concerns of the flesh, and overvalue the relative importance of the things of the spirit. (12–14)

That in his stories Boyesen had few characters who strictly fit
these descriptions may be an indication that his desire was to
avoid such stereotypes. Only Delia Saunders in *The Light of
Her Countenance* fits perfectly one of these, and Boyesen found
that this "personification of the Declaration of Independence,"
this feminist from Indiana, created an uncustomary amount of
controversy: "I was told by a chorus of reviews (and I suspected
the soprano note in most of them) that the type was one of my
own invention; that it did not exist except in my jaundiced eye;
that, if it did exist, I had outrageously caricatured it; and that
I had conclusively proved myself an alien, devoid of sympathy
with the American character" (9). Boyesen reacted defensively to
criticism of his characterization of Delia Saunders: "I had prided
myself on having avoided the farcical exaggerations of my European *confreres.*" Yet readers of *The Light of her Countenance*
are probably correct if they assume that she is much less credible
than Henry James' Henrietta Stackpole, who is surely one of
James' least credible inventions. Usually, however, Boyesen tried
to avoid displeasing his female audience with such stereotypes
of American women. Thus in his heroine-dominated stories and
novels of the 1880s, one finds that when he deviates from the
stereotype, even while avoiding the farcical exaggerations that he
criticizes in European writers, Boyesen fails nevertheless at creating fully individualized human beings. Divorcing the character
from the stereotype allows instead a reversion to the ideal. The

personification of a generalization does not become human, but is turned into a symbol of an abstraction. Sometimes, however, Boyesen nearly succeeds, and these ideal beauties are beguiling despite their unreality.

When he isolates American types, Boyesen becomes the disinterested scientist. His fiction, however, is not scientific; it is the literature of love, and a different spirit prevails. As Wasserstrom explains concerning genteel fiction like Boyesen's: "To my mind, the overriding aim even of genteel fiction—which is very deeply grounded in, yet transcends, moral dualism—is to establish order within the human spirit and in the life of society. What began as an effort to compose sentimental, polite entertainments culminated in a complex literature which portrayed the unity of love and the interrelatedness of love and freedom."[17]

Except for Delia Saunders, most of Boyesen's important female characters of the 1880s represent an attempt to show such unity and interrelatedness. Boyesen's detached criticism, next to his purposeful fiction, indicates an ambivalence about women, especially American women. Yet when he writes fiction it is often apparent that the contradictory nature of women which caused his ambivalence is transformed into a mysterious complexity. The ambivalence is most apparent in the criticism. For example, the second essay in *Literary and Social Silhouettes* compares American and German women, but is inconclusive. Boyesen presents some scurrilous criticism of the American girl here: they are "beautiful little monsters of selfishness and conceit, who at the proper age trip sweetly into matrimony with a thousand demands, and without the least conception of the serious duties which that relation imposes upon them" (27). German women, however, "glory in their domestic martyrdom, their sacrifice of self, their loving and conscientious performance of their duties to husband and children" (30). A few good things are said for the American girl, especially her intelligence and complexity. But the bulk of the essay is negative. Boyesen, however, escapes the dangers of uttering such heretical sentiments by attributing all of these negative statements to a German friend. Without offering a rational argument for his side, Boyesen is arbitrarily pro-American. "But my prejudice (though you may find it hard to believe) is in favor of America and whatever is American" (40).

The essay is thus illogical in its impact. While praising the good wives and mothers of Germany throughout the bulk of the essay, it concludes, for no good reason, that American women are preferable.

III *Nymph and Nun*

Since these antithetical positions are both developed by Boyesen, we might assume that he wants a synthesis of the European and the American woman. Boyesen's later fiction indicates that the best woman is both the archetypal mother-wife and the energetic, complex, and mystifying girl. Interestingly, the aspiring girl and the Western girl are grouped in "Types of American Women" under the single designation American girl. Both types are aggressive, as opposed to the passive German woman. In the essay, the antithetical attributes of the two varieties of American woman were stated in a negative way. One type is sickly, flat-chested, plain, while the other is frenzied, flamboyant, and improper. A combination of the two seems desirable. Give the New England idealist the health, energy, and chest of the Western girl and perhaps then you will have a transcendent woman. Such antitheses—European and American, puritanical and liberated—were juxtaposed in hopes of a transcendent reconciliation in much nineteenth century fiction. A girl should have the mysterious complexity of America and the honest simplicity of Europe. Paradoxically, she should have the innocence of the American while possessing the experience of the European. Yet she should be predominantly American. Freed from traditional restrictions, she can become an individual while performing her sexual role. Somehow she can be both nymph and nun; she can be the Western girl unbound from unhealthy undergarments, free and candid on all topics; and simultaneously she can be the aspiring woman, offering a spiritual example for men, the woman who has renounced vanity and is devoting her life to the pursuit of an ideal.

Yet in typical literature of this sort, the physical qualities of such a girl were submerged, while the spiritual qualities were emphasized. "Though they were accustomed to describe her physical appearance only in order to identify her motives or intimate her latent desires, yet they created a woman who has weight, height, and proportion even though they said very little about her surface. And from the specific images of hair and flowers, occasional references to her figure, a writer masked his physical response to her sheer beauty behind his opinion of her spirit."[18] Here, however, Boyesen differs greatly from most of his contemporaries, for his allusions to a woman's sexuality are not masked. At times he underscores the revealing nature of tight-fitting clothes: "The white cambric negligee clung airily to her form revealing its graceful undulations, the rich hair was twisted into a loose coil on the back of her head."[19] Indeed, the presence of clothing suggests the possibility of its absence: "the fawn colored sack . . . clung to her trim figure as if it were but a divestible epidermis."[20] He concentrates on titillating glimpses of exposed flesh: "Her arms, which were half visible through the sleeves, struck him with wonder, they were so firm and white and the little dimple in the wrist emphasized the perfection of their modeling. The clear, warm shadow of her chin upon the little glimpse of neck which was bared made him almost shiver with delicious appreciation."[21] The diaphanous clothing clings; the body underneath is perfectly modeled, not static, but undulating; the titillating flesh, the arms, the neck, are seen in glimpses.

Even when speaking metaphorically, Boyesen is implicitly sexual. The aspiring woman wore skepticism like a "divestible garment." Boyesen obviously appreciated sensuality. Ordinarily his descriptions of appearances were meant to convey the reality of the character underneath. Just as Boyesen frequently specified class and character through delineation of facial type, Boyesen felt clothes and bodies were expressive: "A woman, with all the spiritual mysteries which that name implies, had always appeared to him rather a composite phenomenon even apart from those varied accessories of dress, in which as by an inevitable analogy, she sees fit to express the inner multiformity of her being."[22]

Boyesen is ambivalent, however, about the attraction of such women. Often he refers to them as madonnas, and often heroes are ready to get down on their knees and worship. But Boyesen retreats from being unabashedly worshipful. Actuality impinges even in those ecstatic moments when heroes propose. Harold Wellingford is ready to fall on his knees before Alma Hampton,

The Daughter of the Philistines, but unfortunately a cab is not
large enough for such chivalry. Boyesen alternates between acceptance of all woman's art as the honest, open expression of
her inner being and skepticism about the femme fatale whose
allure is based on artifice. Does a woman's appearance appeal
to man because it symbolizes what she is or because it contributes
to the enigma?

The tall, lithe magnificence of her form, the airy elegance of her toilet,
which seemed *the perfection of self-concealing art,* the elastic deliber-
ateness of her step—all wrought like a gentle, deliciously soothing
opiate upon the Norseman's fancy and lifted him into hitherto unknown regions of mingled misery and bliss. She seemed a combination
of the most divine contradictions, one moment supremely conscious,
and in the next adorably child-like and simple, now full of arts and
coquettish innuendoes, then again *naive,* unthinking and almost boy-
ishly blunt and direct . . . .[23]

If a woman operates like an opiate upon a man, is she merely
dulling his senses, making her actuality more difficult for him to
perceive, or is she allowing him to retreat into his imagination,
which is the only place where beauty can be known? And what
about this mixture of misery and bliss? Is bliss better unalloyed,
or do pain and pleasure mixed always provide greater joy? When
brought together, the contradictory aspects of woman seem
divine. Boyesen's most simplistic characters in his most simplistic
stories judge women to be either devils or angels. In the very
primitive story, "How Mr. Storm Met His Destiny,"[24] the major
character is unable to reconcile two contradictory views of
woman. Jilted by a woman he loves, Storm gives up his career
in Norway and comes to America. To him all love is folly, the
antithesis of rational behavior, and all women are reprobates.
In his apartment he had painted tiles which depicted Delilah and
other such wicked enchantresses. When the woman who jilted
him, however, leaves her baby by another man at his door with
a note apologizing for her past unfaithfulness and then disappears, Storm recalls his earlier love and begins to search for her.
When he finds her, the lovers are reunited, and the tiles of reprobate women are replaced with Fra Angelicos.

IV   The Light of Her Countenance

Whether the heroine of *The Light of Her Countenance* (1889) is good or evil is not so easily decided. While Constance Douglas by the end of the novel is definitely subject matter for Fra Angelico, until this point we are never really sure. Looked at objectively from a modern point of view, she seems unpromising. She is an expatriate Southern belle who lives in Rome because her gracious America was spoiled by the late unpleasantness. She seems to be a vain woman who devotes her energy and resources to her costumes, and she appears to belong to the most wicked variety of femme fatale, a woman who toys with men's affections and actually drives one man to suicide.

The Light of Her Countenance tells the story of a somewhat decadent, wealthy thirty-year-old American man, Julian Burroughs, who is attempting to find some purpose in his life. After an attempt at politics in which he shows himself to be naive, Julian goes to Europe in quest of a destiny. There he toys with several callings, but finally chooses to pursue a woman, Miss Douglas, in the light of whose countenance he hopes to find meaning. Besides Miss Douglas, as a representative of womanhood, we have Burrough's cousin, Delia Saunders, who gives her life to causes and who, rather inconsistently, ends up marrying an older English aristocrat.

The Light of Her Countenance is representative of Boyesen's heroine-dominated stories, so many of which were written during the 1880s. In a sense it is a failure, a novel which attempts an idealizing of the fashionable lady through sentimental prose, while at the same time employing a good deal of Realistic irony which will not allow any person or thing to be more than what she or it is.

The mixture of styles, sentimental and ironic, is not succesful here. Yet accidentally and unconsciously, Boyesen presents a thematic conflict, represented in these opposing styles, which is similar to that in F. Scott Fitzgerald's *The Great Gatsby*. Without really understanding Constance Douglas, Boyesen seems to have created one of the first bitch goddesses of American art. Daisy Buchanan, followed by a series of Hollywood stars, represents the culmination of this phenomenon, the golden girl of the

golden age who underneath is brass. Daisy is overwhelmed mo-
mentarily by material splendor; clothes—a pile of expensive
shirts—move her to tears. The whole promise of America is
represented in material elegance. Daisy, for all her own wealth,
is drawn by the ostentatious grandeur of Gatsby's house. The
shirts in their redundancy symbolize the poignancy of Gatsby's
quest, which for all its impressiveness, will not sanctify his life
or Daisy's. Constance Douglas is similar. When Julian Burroughs
offers to build his minister friend a church, she is impressed. Her
thoughts are quite Daisylike, because the proposed action is
stirring in scope, like the Buchanan's moving a stableful of polo
horses from Chicago to Long Island. "It seemed a fine thing to
have a lover who could speak of building churches with such
grand *non chalance*."[25] And in a bourgeois way this action,
building churches with money, seems a blending of material and
spiritual.

The Victorian art of dress as presented in this novel reveals
better the sentimental blend of spirit and body which they
achieved. Clothes are to cover nakedness, the Victorians thought,
to hide shame and to bind one. Yet paradoxically, clothes serve a
different function. Surely women who bound themselves up so
tightly, so uncomfortably, were obsessively conscious of the
bodies which they bound. Although Constance Douglas never
weeps over clothes, they obviously have great symbolic value to
her. Boyesen's sentimental, fashion-magazine descriptions indicate that "taste" and "modishness" are part of her ideal nature:

Her toilet gave an impression of combined simplicity and richness
which challenges description. It was not striking, but in admirable
taste, expressing somehow her rare and noble personality in millinery.
A short cloak of blue velvet, edged with swan's down, set off her
fine figure to advantage; and a very modish hat with a pale-blue
feather gave such an effective outline to her head that it seemed
impossible to imagine how she would have looked without it. She
seemed to leave a radiant trail behind her. The impression of her
loveliness was visible as an illumination in everyone's countenance.
(141)

Like Daisy in white, Constance in blue—the Virgin Mary's color—
gives the impression of innocence. Constance Douglas is Amer-

ica's democratic princess, the American girl, who like Grace
Kelly or Christina Light goes to Europe and becomes royalty.
Her laughter may not sound like money, as does Daisy's, but
her appearance, in plumes and velvet, looks like money. Her
figure is "set off," emphasizing her sexuality; her birdlike feathers
are so much a part of her that they convey the intimacy of nakedness. Boyesen understood the function of clothes in the old
dance of love. Therefore it is ironic that Delia Saunders, the
caricatured feminist, embarrasses people with her talk about the
emancipation waist. Nevertheless, Constance Douglas and her
mother feel it necessary to remind Delia that discussion of intimate apparel is not appropriate for mixed company. Yet why is
it inappropriate, why embarrassing? Delia in all her candor is
certainly no bawd. She seems innocent, perhaps asexual, as the
portrait showing her in "a rhetorical attitude with one arm
akimbo and the other extended, as if in passionate remonstrance,"
demonstrates (50). She has rejected being a woman: "Having
committed the mistake of being born a girl, she would do her
utmost to rectify it" (40). The beautiful heathen seems beyond
sexual intrigue, and her marriage at the conclusion of the novel
to the humorously blundering, good hearted, but not particularly
virile middle-aged Englishman seems a Platonic alliance. Embarrassment over the emancipation waist appears to exist because
this healthful, looser undergarment calls attention to the vanity
and purposeful sexuality of the tight-fitting waist which most
women wore. The latter unhealthy garment emphasized womanliness in shape, the narrowness of waist contrasting with an
amplitude of bust and hip, an amplitude which fashion came
to accentuate with bustles.

The characterizations of Constance Douglas and Delia Saunders cause one to wonder how serious Boyesen's commitment
to Realism actually was. The stops are all pulled in describing
Miss Douglas: "But what a transcendent phenomenon she was!"
(135). "She is Circe, the enchantress. Only she does not turn
men into swine, but she turns swine into men" (135). In contrast, Delia, the slander upon American womanhood, is a joke.
Yet she is a teller of truth in the novel. Our approving smiles
are, thus, indulgent, as with a child. She is used to support a
major theme in the novel which is critical of artifice in life and

art. While apparently Boyesen was aware of the dangers of sentimentality and artifice of manners in literature and life, he seemingly preferred all the lies Constance represents to the truth itself, as represented by Delia. He makes Delia Saunders crudely candid. Upon meeting Sir Percy, an English aristocrat, Delia remarks to her cousin Julian: "Jule, isn't it true that a lot of English lords have gone into the dry goods and butcher business in the United States?" (120).

Delia insults people with aplomb, with the rationalization that she is, after all, serving truth. Once she offended the English artist Talbot, and he replied, " 'That isn't exactly complimentary.' . . . She replied, 'It wasn't intended to be complimentary . . . it was intended to be true' "(66). Such candor is refreshing, but we never know whether to be outraged or charmed. Her reaction to the clichés of romance is amusing and seems a direct criticism of the highly sentimental way romantic matters are handled in the rest of the novel. For example, in her proposal scene, she mocks romance:

"Miss Saunders," repeated her visitor with a tremendous effort, as he faced her again, "What a pity—what a pity—that we have hearts."

"Yes," cried Delia, audaciously burlesquing his manner, "and—and—stomachs!" (192)

Who is the object of satire here? Delia for her crude bluntness or Sir Percy for his histrionics? Is this indeed criticism of Julian because of his similarities to Sir Percy? Or is Boyesen belittling a deficiency of style? Sir Percy, after all, in his attempts to be romantic is not suave enough to succeed. Certainly it seems that Delia is honest with regard to sex, while Constance is dishonest. But Boyesen appreciates more the genteel dishonesty than a realistic view of sex. While Delia carries Boyesen's most important theme, she is not to be taken seriously. She is the silly, immature unrefined girl, who is always treated patronizingly in literature and life, while Constance is the sophisticated woman deserving all attention.

As was the case with Olaf Varberg of *A Norseman's Pilgrimage*, it is also difficult to determine what our attitude should be toward the hero, Julian. In both novels the hero is looking toward a woman to achieve some transcendence. Boyesen's tendency to satirize these men indicates his own ambivalence about the redemptive aspects of womanhood. In *The Light of Her Countenance*, Julian's Romanticism must be contrasted with Delia's Realism. Whereas Delia is the stereotyped American whose cause is woman's liberation, Julian is the Europeanized American male who seeks to use woman as a symbol in his quest for a purpose in life. Both face the problem of being self-defeating. Boyesen implies that Delia in fighting for woman's rights is destroying the sense of dignity which in the possession of women gives sovereignty. Certainly Constance Douglas, a traditional woman unconcerned with feminism, seems more powerful than Delia, according to Boyesen's interpretation, in that she has "the ability to melt all discordant social elements into harmony by means of her passive beauty" (136). Julian defeats himself by being ludicrously romantic about his idealized woman, by being too earnest in his quest for purpose in life.

His naive Romanticism about women spills over into his other quests. In hopes of finding meaning, Julian goes into politics and is surprised to discover that he is being used by dishonest politicians, that democracy in his city is sham, and that even if he had won (he did not because his own side defected) it would have been meaningless. In his wanderings in Europe, Julian seeks a life of self-sacrifice, and any self-sacrifice will do since he has no idea of what he should sacrifice himself for. Should he be æsthetic or ascetic? He laments that he had never "eaten dry bread and salt for dinner for weeks, in order to save the money for the purchase of an Etruscan vase or a bronze Bacchante or a rare *intaglio*" (104). He considers becoming a philanthropist or a civil servant: "He would dignify this love of his by making it an inspiration for civic usefulness, for philanthropy and good works. He would rise by means of this love to the full stature of his manhood" (279). At other times Julian considers vaguely, "The higher life—the life of renunciation" (265).

Just as Julian's political venture fails, his other means of justifying himself are discredited. He is clearly not cut out for a life of renunciation; building splendid churches will not allow passage of his camel through the needle's eye; he is not an artist. Even his desire for fulfillment through love is discredited: "Men do not, he reflected, in the nineteenth century start out on a quixotic quest for beautiful women whom they have never seen. . . . He was inclined to believe at times, that he was simply deluding himself, and with the zest for romantic hallucination which is more pardonable at twenty than at thirty, coquetting with feelings which were long since extinct" (102).

Although the novel appears to be a compromise with Philistine values, it aims high. In fact, the pretentiousness of its theme calls attention to its glaringly sentimental bourgeois values. Julian "yearned dimly for some grand passion, which even though it were hopeless, might dignify his existence and reclaim it from its ugliness and base futility" (104). The word "passion" here is ambiguous in its nature, indicating either biological or theological forces. Nineteenth century Americans longed for redemption from "ugliness and base futility," but whether this redemption would be physical or spiritual is difficult to tell. Boyesen, in *The Light of Her Countenance*, lingers fondly on the details of the world the book supposedly condemns. Julian's apartment is fashionably decadent; his manner with his servants, ordering one to remove his moustache, is impressively imperious. The luxurious appointments of his life may be splendid or depraved: "Julian Burroughs was reading in a leather-covered easy chair between a richly draped window and an oaken writing table of elaborate workmanship. A drowsy wood-fire, breaking fitfully into flame, was burning between a pair of artfully twisted brass andirons. It filled the room with its ruddy glow and glistened on the many ornaments, but did not dispel the twilight" (7).

The hint of evil in the lovingly described scene is basic to the whole somewhat decadent tone of the novel, for Boyesen titillates us with material and physical splendor, while advocating renunciation and spiritual otherworldliness. For example, he does not offer redemption alone in the love of a woman; he also offers the excitement of evil. "And opposite to him in the mirror stood she, placid as a goddess, and as unattainable. She was smiling affably—a trifle condescendingly, he thought—and it flashed through his mind that he was but one of a long procession of *victims* who had immolated themselves upon her altar" (127).

What these women who are both transcendent phenomena and cruel enchantresses demonstrate is the impossible dualism of

Boyesen's world. He had no unified sensibility which could create Beatrices or Lauras. The physical could not be sanctified by the spiritual. Yet many Victorians like Boyesen, whose lives were blatantly committed to the material and the physical, hypocritically pretended to reject the body. They were helplessly enthralled by what they believed evil, but to conceal their hysteria, they ritualized contact between sexes. On the surface, the ritual of love had as its basic action the proposal which seemed to reinforce the idea of the purity of woman. The man must humbly offer his love, proclaiming his unworthiness. Always the girl is aware of what is about to happen in the proposal scene. Her face flushes, her agitation becomes visible; often words need not be spoken; and often she rebuffs the proposal before it is offered.

In *The Light of Her Countenance*, Julian must confess his past sins, in his case a love affair which is said to be sordid, although its sordidness is never specified. The pure woman then has the right to be heartless and unforgiving. How dare a soiled man approach her spotless purity? Yet the proposal is also a proposition, and a woman, especially one impressed by wealth as Constance Douglas seems to be, is a whore. She is selling intimacy. Perhaps, then, the punishment dished out by Constance Douglas for the suitor's past sins is transferred guilt; the woman recognizes the sordid role she plays in this transaction, and so she punishes the man, simultaneously punishing herself by depriving herself of what she desires. Perhaps the woman knows she is not as untouched by sin as the myth portrays her, and so she punishes men rather than admit it. It is no wonder then that Constance stresses subtlety; she wishes to avoid the embarrassment of explicitness. Thus, Julian is successful with her because "She had never in her life received homage that seemed so delicate, so unobtrusive and so thoroughly acceptable. . . . All was so harmonious, so civilized" (227).

What is so admirable about Julian is that he appears "polished and self restrained," despite his having a "spark of barbarian untamability, of hot primitive passion, in his blood, which long subjection to social conventions had half smothered" (101). The irony of their love relationship is that while she appreciates the delicate homage that such a polished man offers, both obviously desire the "hot primitive passion" of the blood.

V   *"The Horns of a Dilemma"*

One sees Constance Douglas too much from the outside to accurately judge what purpose Boyesen intended her to serve. He apparently felt that if the reader knew too much about her "underground economies," all mystery would be lost. For comparison, it might be illuminating to look closely at a woman whose inner thoughts about love are represented. Margaret Hungerford, heroine of "The Horns of a Dilemma," is confused about her role in life, spiritual or physical, and her confusion is represented in part by the choice which she has to make between two men.[26] One is tempted in fact to think of the "horns" of the title as a sexual allusion and to see Miss Hungerford's name as a pun (like Lady Wishfort). Miss Hungerford is, however, to her suitors another transcendent phenomenon. She is compared with a madonna; one of the suitors gets down on his knees before her. The heroine is, nevertheless, an American girl who thinks realistically, and whether she wishes to be idealized or not is a puzzle. At one time she inspires poetry in which she is idealized. She is grateful for the immortality she gains and begins to think of herself as a Laura or a Beatrice.

Poetry, she thinks, has weaned her from such unfeminine influences as Spencer and Darwin. Yet when she discovers that the poetry has been written by someone other than the man she had attributed it to, she is forced into a dilemma. Margaret has fallen in love with a man named Northan because she believes that he has celebrated her in verse. In effect, she loves the poetry rather than the man. When she discovers that Sutherland, an effete, less virile, Europeanized man, has written the verse, however, she cannot transfer her affection. Northan's robust American manliness has more to do with her affection than she realized. She finds herself rationalizing in his favor: "it was not his fault if she had persisted in investing him with imaginary attributes" (400). She has beguiled herself with the idea of a Romantic heroine celebrated by a poet, but when the illusion gives way, she shows herself to crave reality more than romance.

Margaret Hungerford is able to rationalize the very realistic physical attraction that she feels for Northan through her powers of refraction, powers so characteristic of Victorian heroines. Nothing at all can be sordid in connection with her:

> Her mind refracted the ordinary moral light of the world into all its beautiful possibilities, tingeing each with a red or blue or yellow halo of sentiment. To be in her presence for ten minutes was like a moral bath. Your sordid self evaporated and you began to feel heroic; all the fine things you once believed yourself capable of, but which through your present cynical spectacles, you looked upon as childish, approached again within the range of possibility. (399)

"The Horns of a Dilemma" is a surprising story because the heroine somewhat enigmatically chooses the coarser man. The author's sympathies seem to be with Sutherland, whose aim it is to understand "the laws which govern this vast cosmic machinery" (390). In comparison, Northan seems loutish; his morality is called into question when he benefits from everyone's mistaken assumption that he has written the Romantic poems which praise the heroine. Yet a heroine such as the one described above serves to redeem appearances, to change what seems a morally compromising situation into something divinely ordained. Ironically, she manages to serve this Romantic purpose best when she makes an uncompromisingly Realistic choice.

VI *Unseemly Predicaments*

Boyesen and his readers evidently enjoyed the titillation derived from unseemly predicaments. In "Swart Among the Buckeyes," the hero carries the heroine, clad only in her nightclothes, through an Ohio town in the middle of the night.[27] In *Falconberg*, much is made of Einar's dishabille in the presence of the saintly Helga after his being hit by a brick. To the sexually squeamish young lady reader, these scenes must have been thrilling and shocking. Yet she could not really disapprove, for after all, they were necessary encounters. In "Swart," melodramatic circumstances in which the heroine had to be physically rescued from the villain point out a kind of excusable, sublimated sex which is found in the typical melodrama. The physical rescue resembles a sexual conquest, yet it is done for the sake of virtue rather than lust.

So we see that often sex in Boyesen is barely camouflaged. No doubt the circumstances of the hero and heroine in "Queen Titania" were titillating to readers.[28] In this story the young lady heroine begins as the adopted child of the hero and ends as his lover and wife. Briefly, the story tells of a young man, Quintus, who adopts a child whom he met on a boat from Europe after the child's mother died in transit. Years later the child grows into a beautiful girl. To a New York society woman who does not know the hero's relation to the girl, the situation appears scandalous. After favoring him with her companionship, she drops him suddenly, and her father, a wealthy publisher, has him removed from his job as an editor. Later this misunderstanding is cleared up, and the publisher's daughter offers to train Titania and present her to fashionable society. Thus a conflict between the innocent girl and the sophisticated society woman develops. Young Titania is determined to keep her innocence, however, and much to her mentor's disapproval, she rejects a wealthy suitor. Out of place in the corrupt world of society, she runs back home to Quintus, during a winter storm. As a consequence, she is ill for months, and Quintus, who is now both father and lover to her, nurses her back to health.

Illnesses, in fact, often offer the opportunity for a man and a woman to have a degree of intimacy. In *Falconberg*, Boyesen places the hero in the heroine's home for his recuperation. Necessity forced such intimacy, since in his condition he could not be moved. Thus Helga played a maternal role for the invalid, just as Quintus here plays a paternal role. Wasserstrom devotes a chapter of *Heiress of All the Ages* to the father-daughter relationship. "Placing a girl within her father's orbit was first of all good politics and only incidentally acute psychology. Yet the relation provided a kind of shorthand through which the two most perplexing qualities in a woman's character—her virtue and her accessibility—were rendered graphic: it guaranteed her lure and did not discredit her honor."[29]

Without Freud's help, the nineteenth century novelist nevertheless often seemed to understand the way in which passion and idealism are mixed in these parent-child relationships.

The girl who beautifully and innocently lighted her father's cigar figured in the American imagination as a person who somehow held the torch of experience but was untouched by its heat. She embodied an excellent solution to the old problem: What is the origin of and what is the proper response to a good woman's sexual attraction? Deciding that the whole matter is rooted in passionately filial women, literature answered the question to its own satisfaction, fulfilled its drive to expose the inner life of its heroines, represented an affinity which everyone recognized, and presented to society a woman whom everybody admired.[30]

What Boyesen accomplished in "Queen Titania" with his father-daughter relationship is similarly complex. With Titania small, he depicts an ideal family relationship. When society becomes critical of the apparently scandalous living arrangement, the reader was ready to leap to defend the innocence of Titania and Quintus. Yet society is right, since what the gossips see is potentially there. When the girl and her foster father marry, however, the implication is that the purest of marriages are based on just this sort of paternal relationship.

If the father-daughter relationship can so elevate a woman, guaranteeing her lure without discrediting her honor, what of the mother-son relationship? Is not motherhood one area of life where a woman can express her sexuality and yet be at the same time innocent? Boyesen has one very Oedipal story, "The Story of a Blue Vein," in which a young man must choose between his real mother and a slightly older girl who has mothered him since he was an infant.[31] When the actual mother, a countess, finds her son after twenty years of separation, he is a student, ambitiously trying to climb from the lower class life that he and his mother-sister substitute, Rikka, live. The countess is afraid to claim her son, because admitting a child whose existence she had hitherto concealed might cause her to be disgraced. It is apparent, nevertheless, that she is jealous of Rikka's relationship with her son, despite her hesitation in recognizing him. "When he came to tell of Rikka's self sacrificing zeal for his welfare, his words grew warmer and more eloquent. He scarcely noticed at first that there was a sudden chill in the Countess' manner at the mention of the girl's name."[32] Simultaneously, it is apparent that Rikka's motherly feeling for the boy has slipped into sexual attraction:

All sorts of strange thoughts invaded her brain, which formerly had no place there. It never occurred to her anymore to pat him on the cheek while he sat studying, or to kiss him when he came home from school; and she surprised herself one day by proposing to hire the garret on the top floor for his bedroom and study. The eagerness with which he accepted the proposition hurt her a little; and when in order to make amends, he kissed her on the cheek, a slight shiver ran through her. She gave a little embarrassed laugh, and the next moment blushed furiously.[33]

The young man, whose position in society has risen naturally—presumably because of the virtues Boyesen believes he possesses through heredity—chooses Rikka over his mother at the end of the story. Because of his superior knowledge and his social position, his mother-son relationship to Rikka is transposed to a father-daughter relationship, the hero now dominant and Rikka subservient.

VII Dominant Males

Such a relationship, in which the male is superior and dominant and the female is childlike and passive, appears, despite Boyesen's critical essays, to be what he idealized. Thus it is easy to understand his almost characterless heroines, who in many stories earn the love of vastly more complicated men. Sophisticated Dr. Swart in "Swart Among the Buckeyes" falls in love with a pathetically naive, unsophisticated, ignorant, sentimental Ohio girl. She has pathos and is genuine; she aspires toward a higher life, but to the reader her dominant characteristic is her dullness. The European peasant girls of "Ilka on the Hill Top," "Annunciata" and "Anastasia"[34] are similarly inferior to their lovers. Their servility, which results from the combined oppression of masculine and aristocratic tyranny, makes them mysterious only in their enigmatic passivity. An American peasant girl in the story "Charity"[35] is of interest only because she possesses some of the saltiness of coastal New England, because she has an independent spirit underneath her skittishly shy exterior. At the beginning of the story, however, Charity's sexual hysteria is revealed when she squeals and drops a platter of dishes because a man looks at her. She lives innocently with an old man, to whom she is not related by blood. To the gossipy world of Poltucket Island, such circumstances appear, of course, quite improper. What Charity becomes to the hero when he marries her is what she had been to the old man—that is, an innocent daughter.

VIII   Daughter of the Philistines

Even in Boyesen's genuine attempts at Realism during the 1880s, it is apparent that his ideal woman was subservient and like a daughter. In *The Daughter of the Philistines* and "A Problematic Character," matriarchal women are discredited and proved immoral, while sweet, passive, daughterly women who stay in their place are praised. *The Daughter of the Philistines* (1883) begins with a few satirical thrusts at Mamma and matriarchy. A girl settles for herself that she will marry, "but leaves the choice of date and victim to Providence and Mamma. If either of these authorities (who in a well-regulated family are nearly synonymous) fails to give satisfaction the time comes for asserting individual preferences. Papa is called in for consultation (which in well-regulated families is a very rare occurence), and rebels mildly against Providence, or rather its synonym."[36]

Mrs. Hampton, Alma Hampton's mother, is like many Boyesen matriarchs. After engineering her husband's success in a small town in the West, she has moved the family against father's will to New York, where she now is engaged in a vicious struggle to climb to the top of society. She is a strong woman, unhampered by any romantic attachments. As a case in point, she has allowed seven of her nine children to die from lack of care. "The fact was, Mrs. Hampton was too occupied with investments, schemes for her social aggrandizement, and even active speculation, to have much time to devote to her children" (18). It is this uncaring woman who presides over the disintegration of her family. Her son becomes dissolute; her daughter must be dropped because of her unfashionable marriage; her husband is caught in his own tainted stock speculations and becomes bankrupt. She, however, survives the misery and loss and, once her husband is dead, goes off to Paris with enough reserves of her own to live in considerable style. The family life over which she presides is cold; the luxurious house is comfortless, as Alma discovers when once, after a marital spat, she returns: "Heart-sick and miserable, she wandered away through the magnificent spacious halls, the walls of which during the last year had been inlaid with complex figures of green, red, and yellow marble" (229).

Alma is trained to follow in her mother's footsteps, but miraculously, the daughter of the Philistines is changed through her choice of husband, Harold Wellingford, a geologist. Mrs. Hampton had not approved of Wellingford as a suitor because he was not rich. But Alma has gone ahead and married him anyway, although her reasons for her choice are little better than her mother's objections. Wellingford's looks are more important at first to Alma than either his intelligence or his character. In marriage Alma is at first quarrelsome, refusing to understand that the Wellingfords cannot afford to live as extravagantly as the Hamptons do. A crisis in the marriage develops when Alma wants to accept some money that a gentleman friend has won for her through stock speculation. Wellingford lectures his wife at this point on the evils of playing the market.

Other didactic moments occur in the novel when Wellingford finds it necessary to lecture his wife on other topics. He speaks as Boyesen's persona, and thereby the author is able to assume a fatherly relationship with his predominantly female reading audience. Charming as Alma and the young lady readers are, Boyesen assumes that most of them will always be daughters of the Philistines, and as daughters they must be schooled. Alma in many ways is the eternal little girl. When she attempts to learn about some of her husband's intellectual interests, delving into Darwin, she finds that she is not mature enough to understand. Instead she is distraught by the impropriety of books which discuss the mating of horses and donkeys. Childishly she breaks into tears because of her inability to comprehend this vastly more sophisticated world. This is her first lesson in humility, a killing blow to her matriarchal instincts. Like a child aiming at self-improvement, she makes resolutions: she will not indulge herself in tantrums; she will do her own marketing; she will sell her jewelry to get a "stylish liveried negro"; and she will be "more intellectual" (164). After reading George Eliot and missing the point, "she resolved, among other things, to live a life of humility and devotion, dress in penetential gray woolens, like Dorothea in *Middlemarch*" (168). It is no wonder that heroines like Alma here, and Helga in *Falconberg*, are not prepared for and must be protected from *Madame Bovary* by Boyesen heroes who sedulously keep Flaubert from feminine eyes.

The helplessness of the girl is stressed in *The Daughter of the Philistines* just as it was in "Queen Titania." In both stories we have scenes in which young damsels, alone at night in New York streets during a storm, are overwhelmed by their circumstances. Similarly, a subplot in *The Daughter of the Philistines*, in which a Jewish girl named Rachel is abducted by Walter Hampton, emphasizes the helplessness of the girl. The Jewish girl is passive, like Boyesen's wondrous European peasants, and it is apparent that the author admires her greatly. Rachel's standards are, "I only know that a woman should be quiet and obedient" (193). The subplot seems to have been added mainly to contrast Jewish patriarchy with New York society matriarchy.

Despite its condescension, *The Daughter of the Philistines*, written considerably earlier than *The Light of Her Countenance*, is much more successful than the later novel in its characterization of an American girl. The success here lies in the way in which irony is dominant in the treatment of the heroine, while sentimentality is minimized. In a sense, Boyesen allows the reader to be beguiled, just as Wellingford and his family are beguiled, before ironically demonstrating Alma's limitations. One learns first that Alma is an exceptional beauty, that she is thus a social asset to her mother. Alma's stylishness is evidently something to be appreciated; it indicates how she represents harmony and order. Only later, when the reader discovers that Alma has used up her allowance, does one realize that she has spent a great deal on clothes. Then in retrospect the initial appreciation of her stylishness seems sentimental. Never in Boyesen's characterization of Constance Douglas is the fashionable aspect of the character shown as being inconsistent with the idealizing of her by her suitors. Had Boyesen used irony more effectively, he might have made Constance a believable woman who though diminished in power was more real, more worthy of love, though not of worship.

IX "A Problematic Character"

The contrast between artful evil women who try to dominate
and guileless good women who accept their place is also developed in "A Problematic Character." Here Boyesen reverses
his standard approach to the international novel, becoming more
like James or Howells. Instead of America symbolizing imaginative freedom as it did so often in his emigrant stories, America
in this novella is cramped, puritanical, and unstimulating, whereas Europe represents its opposite. Europe also, however, represents sin, and Boyesen prefers America to that.

His two female characters, between whom the hero must
choose, are Alice Beach, a Puritan New Englander whose "un-
compromising frankness and honesty seemed to radiate from
every line and feature,"[37] and "Madame Valerie de Salincourt,
fresh from Parisian salons,"[38] whose manners are flamboyant and
calculatingly artful. Madame de Salincourt is not entirely de-
spicable. In fact, her mythically evil past, which Boyesen refrains
from specifying throughout the first installment, makes her much
more interesting than Alice, the "staunch little utilitarian." Alice's
innocence makes madame want to weep at her own worldly
depravity. Only when he sees the aging European woman's
machinations to steal Hannibal, a young artist, away from Alice,
does the reader perceive how deep her evil goes. Hannibal, after
rejecting her, makes the definitive judgment: "She is impressive
yet, and she never will be anything but interesting. Her honesty,
however, is problematic, and the archness which was charming
at twenty-eight loses some of its fascination at thirty-two."[39]

X Daughters and "Iron Madonnas"

Boyesen obviously was still trying during the 1880s to achieve
some sort of reconciliation through his characterization of women.
Like his reunions of fathers and sons in immigrant stories, his
father-daughter marriages offer a way of blending worlds: here
one is spiritual, the other physical. Such daughterly heroines can
hardly be individualized. Instead their role is that of the idealized Romantic heroine. The choice which lovers must make
between women, when one is subservient and the other is matriarchal, is obviously a crucial moral one. It is a choice between

all that is fitting and proper—which, for Boyesen, a male-dominated world apparently exemplifies—and the perverse and unnatural order which he seems to feel feminine rule embodies. Yet Boyesen supposedly believed in evolution, and according to his Spencerian principles, women should be striving toward individual identity: "By the same inscrutable processes of growth which impel all creation towards its divine goal, woman is bound to develop the potentialities of her nature and assume more important functions for which her talents may fit her."[40] Later Boyesen heroines do strive to develop their individual characters. During the 1880s, however, the only powers Boyesen saw women as possessing were negative. Besides their matriarchal tendencies in adulthood, the younger woman exercised too much influence over American letters. The arbiters of the novelist's fate in America were young ladies "whose opinions on any other subject involving the need for thought or experience, we should probably hold in light esteem." The American girl is the "Iron Madonna who strangles `in her fond embrace the American novelist; the Moloch upon whose altar he sacrifices willingly his chances for greatness."[41]

An "Iron Madonna" is an alloy of spiritual and physical. Here, however, Boyesen seems aware that the mixture is deadly; Miss America represents rank bourgeois sentimentalism. Boyesen later turned to a more sophisticated Romanticism, perhaps a quasi-Naturalism, where a grand theory, evolution, demanded that his characters be developed as individuals. Whether Boyesen's Realistic characterizations, once free of his sentimental prejudices, are fit enough to survive is a matter still to be investigated.

CHAPTER 5

The Theorist and The Realist

I Boyesen and Howells: What Realism Is

HJALMAR Hjorth Boyesen possessed in his theories all of
the attributes of the Realistic writer, although he did not
have these in the same balance and proportion that Howells
had. Howells recognized Boyesen as his staunchest theoretical
ally, but one might infer from Howells' remarks about Boyesen's
support that he wished it had been somewhat less strenuous.
"Boyesen, indeed, out-realisted me, in the polemics of our
aesthetic, and sometimes when an unbeliever was by, I willingly
left to my friend the affirmation of our faith, not without some
quaking at his unsparing strenuousness in disciplining a heretic."[1]
Howells, whose own literary career indicates he had a large
tolerance for ideas at variance with his own, was embarrassed by
Boyesen's doctrinaire support. It seems that where Howells in
defending Realism was being positivistic, accepting science as
the end of philosophy, and attempting to find a pragmatic literary method for a world where sensate experience is all we can
know, Boyesen was defending Realism as a new philosophy, a
way in which scientific law was to explain the mystery of life.
What was a sophisticated literary method to Howells was a
key to ultimate truth to Boyesen. Boyesen was, therefore, an
enthusiast of the Realists' faith, while Howells was but an
advocate.

Their respective reactions to past and new literary modes indicate their differences in zeal. Howells' rejection of Romanticism
was not as strenuous or as arrogant as that of Boyesen. He saw
it merely as a formerly vital literary movement which had
become outmoded: "The romantic of that day and the real of
this are in a certain degree the same. Romanticism then sought,
as realism seeks now, to widen the bounds of sympathy, to level

102

every barrier against aesthetic freedom, to escape from the paralysis of tradition. It exhausted itself in this impulse."[2] Howells sensibly viewed the history of literature in terms of waves which replace each other but do not necessarily progress further upon the sands. "When realism becomes false to itself, when it heaps up facts merely, and maps life instead of picturing it, it will perish too."[3] Such wisdom allowed Howells, while disturbed about the pessimism and impropriety of early Naturalism, to understand why Norris and others were attempting their more vivid pictures. Realistic pictures were losing their clarity, becoming outlines or merely maps of experience in the chaotic world of the 1890s. Cosmic outlines became necessary if a picture of reality were to have any coherence.

On the other hand, Boyesen's view of literary history was evolutionary and progressive. Realism was an evolutionary stop beyond Romanticism. Boyesen was given to hyperbolic statements, attributing to Romantic literature a sort of diabolic power which could destroy democracy. Boyesen, like Mark Twain, who jokingly blamed the Civil War on Sir Walter Scott, saw the medieval values of Romantic literature as dangerous to democracy. He blamed the prevalence of romances in young ladies' libraries for the sham British type aristocracy found in New York, feeling that such non-American attitudes would enervate and ultimately destroy American democracy, which depends upon purposeful individual initiative.[4] In advocating a copyright law, in fact, he argued that the law was essential to the survival of American democracy because without such a law America would continue to be flooded with English romances.[5] To Howells Realism was principally a method which was to be employed to awaken the consciences of his readers by its fresh point of view. To Boyesen, Realism was a new form of propaganda, working for democracy as Romanticism had worked for feudalism. While Howells was concerned mainly with the individual consciences of his readers, Boyesen was concerned with the outcome of society. The Romance was something that had once been appropriate, according to Howells, for handling those personal problems which are at the same time universal problems. To Boyesen the Romance had always been a failure. It was no wonder that in writing about "The Evolution of the

Heroine" he was such a poor literary historian. His cosmic view
would not allow eighteenth century fiction to be more Realistic
than early nineteenth century fiction. Hence, he erroneously
would assume that Scott is an improvement on Richardson in
terms of psychological Realism. Just as in political history man
was evolving toward greater democracy, in literature Boyesen's
belief required that he was moving toward greater Realism.

Although Boyesen did not live as long into the period of
Naturalism as Howells did, one can see that here too Boyesen
lacked the openness and geniality toward new developments
which characterized Howells. Neither Howells' optimism—which
had been blunted by certain unhappy events—nor his prudish-
ness precluded his making accurate aesthetic judgments, for
neither was part of any larger systematic view of reality. One
accepts and ultimately overlooks the fact that Howells both sees
the subject matter of *Anna Karenina* as inappropriate for American audiences and simultaneously praises the novel with inspiring extravagance.[6] Boyesen, who was not hesitant in admiring
literature which handled sex with relative candor, allowed theory
to dominate over aesthetic judgment. Hence we find him preferring the less significant to the more significant, Bjørnson to
Ibsen, Daudet to Zola, because he shared Bjørnson's and Daudet's view of reality. In retrospect, Boyesen's mistakes in judgment seem naive in the same way that Marxist prescriptions
about what literature should be seem naive. Yet in his time,
when literature was discredited by pragmatism, when novel
reading seemed a vice, Boyesen's efforts to place fiction on the
respectable bandwagon of science were noble. Howells too was
interested in associating literature with science, and so it appears
that they marched in the same cause for a while, although, one
should note, to different drums.

If one compares their major critical documents, Boyesen's
Literary and Social Silhouettes and Howells' *Criticism and Fiction*, one finds, as literary historians who appear to have read
only this one work by Boyesen have found, that Boyesen enu-
merated the same critical principles as did Howells. It is only
when one understands how much Boyesen yoked together in
linking science to Realism—an understanding which comes
from reading his critical essays on contemporary Europeans

and from a perusal of his last novels—that one sees that Boyesen had something else in mind than Howells did when he spoke of Realism. Boyesen's novels differ from Howells' because of his different perception of the relation between science and Realism. As a consequence, he was writing in a somewhat different genre from that of Howells.

For both Howells and Boyesen, Realism is a mimetic theory of art in which that actuality which is verifiable by experience is depicted rather than an internal imaginative world. In accordance with this theory, they attempted to avoid artifice in structuring their works; both the imposition of Classical rules and the subjective form giving of Romantic inspiration were seen as falsifications of reality. They believed that art should approximate life itself. In duplicating real life, the writer in a predominantly middle class democracy should write about average people rather than a mythical nobility. He should document the life and problems of his culture. Thereby, he does not provide man with an entertaining escape from his world but turns his attention toward it. Such literature thus serves an important role in society; it awakens individual consciences and causes men to contemplate realistically the world as it is. Well-defined problems, therefore, will cry out for reform.

This definition of Realism, it should be emphasized, stresses the affective aspects of literature. Both Boyesen and Howells wrote with their audiences in mind; both recognized that young girls were the arbiters of the novelist's fate in America. In addition, American writers worked in a nation which for Puritan reasons doubted the value of art, fearing entertainments because nothing that was not sinful was done merely for pleasure. Under such circumstances, a writer was bound to desire to be useful. To present truth to the multitudes was to serve a social purpose.

The concept of Realism, as we see, is predicated upon a belief in the existence of a particular type of material appropriate to art in a modern bourgeois democracy, an assumption that the artist has limits and responsibilities as interpreter of these materials, and a conviction that literature is useful in affecting the sensibilities of its readers. In all of these aspects, the views of Boyesen and Howells were similar enough to make Boyesen appear to be giving Howells support. For example, Boyesen's criticism of novelists like Wilkie Collins and Gaboriau for ransacking "the records of police courts and lunatic asylums in search of startling incidents"[7] seems a direct reinforcement of Howells who, in order to be true to American "well-to-do actualities," was willing to take "the risk of being called commonplace."[8]

While their definitions of Realism are similar, there are significant differences. Howells' definition of realism as "nothing more and nothing less than the truthful treatment of material"[9] is an annoying truism which, despite its initial claim of precision, tells us nothing more than we already guessed and leaves us with nothing less than a description which applies to the majority of art. Boyesen's most important statement concerning Realism goes further than this and yet simultaneously qualifies any claim of precision by placing his definition in the category of those "broadly" spoken. Besides, he defines the artist of the movement rather than the movement itself. "Broadly speaking, a realist is a writer who adheres strictly to the logic of reality, as he sees it; who, aiming to portray the manners of his time, deals by preference with the normal rather than the exceptional phases of life, and, to use Henry James' felicitous phrase, arouses not the pleasure of surprise, but that of recognition."[10] The definition Boyesen gives is one which could easily have been given by Howells, yet since it is known to whom each statement can be attributed, it is profitable to see where the emphases and where the ambiguities lie. While Howells talked a great deal about the appropriate material for Realistic writing, what ultimately distinguished Realism from other types of writing for him was the treatment. Boyesen, however, put major emphasis on the selection of material to be treated, believing that in actuality there was only one logic of reality and that a writer must choose his material in order to reveal it.

II *How Literature Teaches*

Literature, Boyesen believed, functioned to teach man what reality is, how to recognize it, and how to adapt to it. Knowledge of reality, to begin with, was not a metaphysical matter. Man knew the world as he adapted to it. Modern science, however, had uncovered in the theory of evolution the key to adaptation. In an essay on Alexander Keilland, Boyesen said that "Success is but adaptation to environment, and success is the supreme aim of the modern man. The authors who, by their fearless thinking and speaking, help us toward this readjustment should, in my opinion, whether we choose to accept their conclusions or not, be hailed as benefactors."[11] Yet it is questionable whether Boyesen would hail a man as a benefactor whose conclusions he had chosen not to accept.

Boyesen was never very specific in explaining how technically one helped a reader toward readjustment. Primarily, it appears that literature served this function best when it dished up experience to the reader whole, in order that he "seem to live the story rather than read it."[12] The aim was that "The literary medium disappears and Nature rises out of the book with her august and terrible countenance. . . . Such books, whether they be novels or plays, *become experiences*."[13] In effect, such works necessitate "a new adjustment of our attitude toward life."[14] The naivete of such a point of view rests in Boyesen's assumption that all men will learn the same thing from experience. If such were the case, literature would not be necessary as an intermediary. In a sense, Boyesen, the arch antiromantic, is espousing an aspect of Romanticism found in optimistic Darwinism—that is, the belief that men and society, once shameful artifice is stripped away, will recognize the true and will consequently move to a higher stage of evolution.

Part of Boyesen's interpretation of experience and literature, however, depended on his classical concept of order. Therefore, Boyesen objected to the pessimistic scientific views of Zola and the unrestrained individualism of Ibsen and Nietzsche.[15] In rejecting such writers of the continental avant garde, Boyesen argued simultaneously and somewhat illogically that the reality of the modern world was self-apparent. Actually, although Boyesen asked that literature be natural like experience, he desired and found most charming in works he criticized not naturalness but "a certain richness of temperament on the author's part, which suffuses even the harshest narrative with a rosy glow of hope."[16] Boyesen seems unconscious at this point that the "rosy glow," like Hawthorne's firelight or Coleridge's "accidents of light and shade," transforms such so-called "real" experiences.

Thus it appears that not only should man interpret experience under this rosy glow, but he should also be aware that experience demonstrates certain political truths which were dear to Boyesen. He felt that once man saw evolution in all life, he should keep certain ultimates in mind. To him, for example, Goethe's *Faust* represented an attempt to show "that the individual exists for the benefit of the race."[17] If evolution has one lesson, it is that in the conflict of finite and infinite, the finite is inadequate to fulfill the aspirations of the infinite. Therefore, Boyesen lauded Realistic and Naturalistic developments in literature as long as they demonstrated that the individualism of Romanticism was tamed and curbed in the representative figure. Consequently, Boyesen was critical of a writer like Brandes who "has so profound an admiration for the man who dares to rebel that he fails to do justice to the motives of society in protecting itself against him."[18] On the other hand, Boyesen praised Bjørnson because he emphasized that individuals should bend their own desires to conform with the good of society.[19]

That Boyesen's idea of Realism depended both upon the selection of material and upon the attitude taken toward this material, but not really on the treatment of material, explains how he could write such sentimental romances after having supposedly accepted Turgenev as his mentor in 1874. *A Norseman's Pilgrimage* after all presents photographic views of German cities and Norwegian country life, in addition to documenting the conflicting attitudes of Europe and America. *Falconberg* provides a glimpse of Midwestern immigrant life, discusses politics and journalism, and demonstrates a strong man's struggle for success. *A Daughter of the Philistines* shows us New York society and Wall Street financial life, demonstrating how man's energies are being diverted into an unproductive struggle for success in both. *The Light of Her Countenance* presents further Realistic views of politics and additional travel material. Boyesen's adherence to the "logic of reality" in

barbaric swamp from which modern man struggled to emerge; to Adams medievalism represented man's last moment of harmonious life. Boyesen believed that in order for democracy to succeed, man must make the inner life secondary and the outer life primary; he was obsessively concerned with man's fulfilling his social obligations. Adams, on the other hand, believed that a means by which the inner life can survive in the face of the demands of a self-destroying society must be discovered. Adams found himself living two irreconcilable lives, one public and the other private. He wrote:

> But we, who cannot fly the world, must seek
> To live two separate lives; one in the world
> Which we must ever seem to treat as real;
> The other in ourselves, behind a veil
> Not to be raised without disturbing both.[1]

It is that private life which the compromises of democracy so imperil. Madeline, the heroine of Adams' novel *Democracy*,[2] goes to Washington to touch with her own hand the massive machinery of society and discovers humans powerless in its presence. In Boyesen's similar story concerning innocence corrupted by power in Washington, *The Golden Calf*, the hero finds the hugeness and machinelike quality of the city world inspiring. It is self-serving individualism which destroys, not the machine of society. Boyesen seems to accept all the implications of modern industrial society sanguinely.

Boyesen, a man whose private life was committed to public appearance, obviously felt that obsessive self-concern was an evil which had lingered on after the demise of Romanticism. His desire for a home life of stately appearances and a professional life of manifold public reward indicates willingness on his part to subordinate the internal to the external. For Adams, whose intellectual inheritance included Puritanism and Romanticism, it was paramount that the internal self be kept alive for introspection and imagination even at the expense of public failure.

II *Democracy and the Industrial Revolution*

Boyesen's essay "The Hope of Nations" published in the *Inde-*

pendent, a New York newspaper of a Christian viewpoint, is representative of Boyesen's political ideas.[3] Its placement in this paper indicates also how much Boyesen's views and those of progressive Christianity coincided. The article denounces a reversion to barbarism which Boyesen saw in the buildup of arms and armies in France and Germany. Modern nations which engage in such dangerous causes of pride are still under the baleful influence of monarchism rather than the salubrious influence of democracy. Interestingly, for Boyesen it is democracy's marriage to the industrial revolution which makes its influence so healthful: "A true democracy can only exist in an industrial state of society..." (67). It is irrational, romantic monarchies which cause wars to exist. "Kings lean upon armies and bayonets are the foundations of thrones" (67). America is more likely to eliminate war because "The center of gravity in the state, which determines its attitude, rests here with the industrial class, which has everything to lose and nothing to gain by the unsettling and destruction of values which war produces" (67). Optimistically Boyesen proclaims that "Industrial forces unite with moral forces and mutually they advance each other" (67).

His most succinct statement of the benefits of industrialism appears in his essay "Mars and Apollo." European states seemed martial in spirit to Boyesen while America did not. "Ours is an industrial civilization, and emotions which are the products and supports of feudalism cannot long survive where all normal agencies of life tend toward their suppression."[4] The type of progress of which Boyesen spoke was material progress. As mankind, through technological advancement, became more adept at providing greater comfort for the majority of its people, the medieval feudalistic "picturesque spectacle" would lose its value for everyone but a conservative aristocracy.

Buttressing himself with the story of Philemon and Baucis from Goethe's *Faust*, Boyesen discussed his lack of sympathy with those who oppose the advances of industrialism in an essay entitled "Victims of Progress," which also appeared in the *Independent*.[5] Baucis and Philemon were opposed to Faust's scheme to use the location of their mountaintop home for the construction of an astronomical observatory which supposedly would benefit all mankind. To Baucis and Philemon, Goethe's Faust was an evil wizard who "Offered up human sacrifices in the night to strange gods" (610). But as Boyesen and all other readers of Goethe know, "Faust's sleepless desire and dominating passion at this final stage of his career was to benefit humanity" (610). Hence it is necessary to cast some aside. "The path of progress is strewn with victims whose only fault was that they were super-fluous—that the life blood of the age did not pulsate in their brains; they are waste tissue in the body social and would as such (unless they are carried off) impede the vital circulation" (610). As the metaphor indicates, Boyesen did not see any oppo-sition between industrialism and nature. Instead, resistance to such scientific progress is thought unnatural. Despite their being admirable people, Philemon and Baucis do not serve the body social and must be eliminated.

III   *Boyesen's Idea of Progress and its Mythology*

The progress of which Boyesen spoke was always of the prag-matic, prosaic variety. It meant basically the provision of great comforts for a greater number of people. Such progress would of necessity be victorious over the quaint or picturesque. Yet Boyesen, pragmatic as he was, recognized that progress needed its own mythology. The world cannot just be leveled and then that level raised. There must be something which inspires us to raise it. In theory that force was evolution, but as an artist tra-ditionally schooled, Boyesen recognized a need to personify his generalizations. Hence, in writing glowingly about his improving world, Boyesen constantly attributed mythological importance to that which he described. It was a world in which the enlight-ened force of Apollo was replacing the barbaric force of Mars. The Chicago World's Fair of 1893, at which the accomplishments of industrialism were magnificently displayed, was a tremendous inspiration to Boyesen. He called the fair "A New World Fable," proclaiming that the Greeks would have made a legend of it.[6] Industrialists were the new Titans. "All the glorious products of loom and forge, of brain and brawn were heaped up in the White City by the much-resounding lake" (173). This was undoubtedly proof of progress, since "such a wealth of achievement— artistic, mechanical and scientific—has probably never been seen before

in such circumscribed space" (176). The fair was Classical to
Boyesen; its architecture, in fact, was Greek revival. This reversion to Classicism was to Boyesen proof of the meritorious advances provided by industrialism. What if, he asked himself,
the planners had chosen Victorian Gothic architecture? The fair
then would have been a "petrified nightmare," a "riot of un-
fettered imagination" (176).

IV *Universities—Classic Rather than Medieval*

In a similar manner, Boyesen believed that universities succeed
to the extent that they are servants of something both modern
and classical and fail to the extent that they perpetuate medievalism. In his observations about student life in European universities, Boyesen ordinarily denounced the lingering medievalism
he so often found. In German universities, which he generally
favored, he noted that barbaric dueling was still practiced among
students.[7] He lamented that the University of Rome, in medieval
fashion, could not yet separate education from the clergy and as
a consequence stood against all the nineteenth century advances.
At Rome "All natural phenomenon must be studied in connection
with the existence of God," he complained.[8] Thus the university
was parochial, lacking in cultural sophistication, incapable of
philosophical thought, forcing its students to remain children.
Perhaps because of his hatred of almost everything English,
Boyesen reserved his most acid criticism for Oxford and Cambridge. They "are not universities in the modern sense and
scarcely profess to encourage independent research or to assist
in widening the domain of human knowledge."[9] They may have
magnificent endowments, he said, but "the smallest German university with its underpaid professors and half-starved tutors
accomplishes more for the cause of learning."[10]

In some German institutions and in young American universities, Boyesen found an exciting modern mood. Boyesen noted
in the University of Berlin a competitive atmosphere which
fostered excellence. In comparison to most American schools,
which had few distinguished men, Berlin had important progres-
sives such as Fichte, Schleirmacher, and Helmholz.[11] American
professors, Boyesen said, were so often men who had failed else-

where. What Boyesen admired most about German education was the extent to which the scientific method was applied to all knowledge. Instead of chairs held by mediocre men who resist progress, the German system promoted those who best served knowledge. Yet, there is a contradiction in this paean to education of the scientific, industrial age. Boyesen lamented a lack of color in these institutions of Germany and at times indulged himself with fanciful reveries about certain medieval qualities which remained in some institutions.

The University of Chicago and Cornell University received extensive praise as institutions of the scientific, industrial age. Both institutions were founded to encourage innovation and devised to promote public interest in educational endeavors. While Boyesen did not note the parallel with the modern industrial corporation, he praised both Chicago and Cornell for their evident concern with public relations.[12] Professors had to be good salesmen, competing with other salesmen to sell their product to students. The university should please its public by proving its usefulness to its community.

Of these two institutions, Cornell seemed to Boyesen the most innovative. Unlike a European university, Cornell offered instruction in almost any field of study. Its founder, Ezra Cornell, who knew no Latin or Greek, emphasized practical learning—agriculture, mechanical arts, and military tactics. The institution pursued the idea that education of a practical nature could be a panacea for society's ills. Boyesen was equally impressed by Chicago, referring to its founding as a full-grown Minerva birth unknown in the history of education. Chicago, with its large extension program, was representative to Boyesen of the way in which American universities seemed more integrated into the culture and were democratizing.

Boyesen's admiration of the progressive nature of such new American institutions would not have extended to developments at Chicago over the past few decades or to the radical changes at Cornell in the late 1960s. The democratic, industrialized model for education was not, to Boyesen, a system open to free-wheeling individualism. He was sympathetic with the idea behind the land grant institutions which were to be servants of the society which financially supported them.

Boyesen was an enthusiastic supporter of the Chautauqua movement as something democratizing also. Like his own journalistic criticism, the movement was a means by which all could share in the advancement of culture. The aim of the movement was to realize an idea of human brotherhood. Boyesen admired the effort which aimed at bringing "science and literature together to the support of Christianity."[13] But he could not help but worry about the shallowness of many of the Chautauqua lectures and the fact that the audience seemed to prefer entertainers to speakers of substance. Yet he was convinced that even if the lectures were superficial, they lifted lives out of the routine of mere struggling for bread. That was proof enough that they do good.

V The Uses of Literature

In essays on "The Ethics of Robert Browning"[14] and "The Problem of Happiness,"[15] Boyesen demonstrated his own ideas about the uses of literature. In "The Problem of Happiness," he praised Goethe's *Faust* because in the end Faust gave up his Satanic individualism and achieved a better kind of happiness, providing in a tract of land for the "habitation of generations" yet unborn. "I can scarcely conceive of a nobler happiness," said Boyesen, "than that of Faust, when blind and old; he stands on his tower, seeing in spirit the blessings which his labors will confer upon millions of his fellowmen" (1458).

Happiness, Boyesen maintained, is only discovered in submission to duty, and therein is the lesson which George Eliot teaches in *Romola* and *Daniel Deronda*. The unworthiness of Romola's husband does not absolve "her from her duty as his wife" (1458). Boyesen noted that the same message is delivered to Gwendolin under similar circumstances in *Daniel Deronda*. Duty encounters her in Deronda's person, He "for whose approval she hungers, pronounces again the inexorable law—there is no happiness to be found in escape from duty. . . . Society joins in enforcing the moral law by which it can alone exist" (1458).

Placed alongside those who rebel against duty are the romantic rebels, Shelley and Browning.

The pervading note in Shelley is a breathless and utterly lawless
aspiration. . . . (1458) That society has any claim upon the individual
and may justly demand a certain degree of respect for its convictions
and usages, seems never to have occurred to Shelley, and that the
social code of morals, no matter how oppressive in individual cases,
has, and must always have, a certain rationality, was an idea he
utterly scouted. (1458)

Boyesen had praise for Tennyson, but curiously he seemed to
be on the side of cruel nature which Tennyson criticizes in *In
Memoriam*: "So careful of the type she seems./So careless of
the single life."[16] On the contrary, to Boyesen, the problem of
happiness is solved by bending one's passions to the demands
of nature and society, which seemed to be one and the same.
Boyesen, as an immigrant working his way up in American society, often felt the hand of necessity pushing him. It is significant
that he gave this necessity some sanctification—indicating that
society makes legitimate demands on us.

Like Shelley's, the characters of Robert Browning seem to
have no "sort of consciousness of their obligations as members
of society."[17] Boyesen lamented that "moral obligations sit lightly
on this poet" (1595). Yet in his discussion of Browning we are
made aware of all that Boyesen's society demands that one give
up. Browning "delights so in exhibitions of the blood-red barbaric streaks in the human soul that I almost fancy virtue, duty
and all pale abstractions that pull in the opposite direction
affecting him (in this mood) with a certain impatience. They
are less interesting, less picturesque" (1595). Browning's most
"resplendent characterizations" are of those individuals who are
guilty. "All exhibitions of unrestrained energy, concentrated in
a moment of supreme action, are to him beautiful. Happiness—
individual well being—appears the legitimate object of human
pursuit, and his heart warms toward the man or woman who,
instead of sipping it in slow dribblets, drains it in one swift,
glorious draught" (1595).

VI *Restricting Immigration*

At times Boyesen's defense of the necessity of society doing
what it will to protect itself from the excesses of individualism

seems to a modern reader to have an ugly racist aspect to it. Boyesen was very willing to generalize about the national character types of people—speaking always as if somehow his bald statements were the result of some sociological study. Boyesen's generalizations about racial stereotypes, however, seem to have come off the top of his Nordic head, and despite his great belief in being rational, they seem at best ethnocentric. For example, he can say with apparent aplomb, "The sturdy steadfastness and selfrestraint of the Anglo Saxon may be made to furnish a capital foil to the fiery instability and passionate rashness of the Slav and the juvenile light-heartedness and irascibility of the Italian."[18] Hence Boyesen, in his writing on immigration, opposed bringing in people who were to his mind too alien for the predominantly northern European character of America. He saw America as making a dangerous mistake in allowing in people who would become disappointed and enemies of the state. "The Slavs and Magyars have contributed," he maintained, "to anarchy."[19] All immigrant groups, Nordic or southern and eastern European, must become subservient to the American ideal. They could not remain isolated in ethnic communities without doing damage to the nation as a whole. Hence in some essays he was critical of the narrowness of the Norwegian Lutheran Church for keeping its people Norwegian and church-oriented rather than encouraging them to become American and secular. Ultimately Boyesen came to disapprove of almost all immigration, whatever the culture of the immigrants. The consequences of immigration were the despoiling of "the prosperous for the benefit of the unprosperous."[20]

That society needs to protect itself from the excesses of the Romantic individual is apparent in Boyesen's ideas about education, immigration, and literature, yet within each area there is always an inconsistency. In education, for example, he could not help but admire the picturesque quality of the medievalism which he found in theory to be so dangerous. Even in his ethnocentric discussion of the northern European, one senses, especially in a slumming episode toward the end of *Social Strugglers*, that he craved some of the hot-blooded passion which he attributed to other so-called inferior cultures. And after having damned Browning at some length for his immoral excesses, Boyesen came to the questionable conclusion that Browning was the greatest living poet. Paradoxically, Browning receives highest praise for just those aspects which Boyesen had condemned.

VII *Inconsistencies: Truth Versus the Picturesque*

Boyesen's inconsistency is most apparent in his attitude toward detail. He nearly always interrupted his paeans to the truth of science to insert an interesting detail. That detail is always quaint, romantic, anachronistic, or irrational. It is as if he believed his system of generalizing was incompatible with art, that instead one could only slip one's cold, general, scientific truths unobtrusively into charmingly told anecdotes. On a topic such as education at the University of Rome, Boyesen deviated from his purported thesis to lament the loss of medieval color.

Boyesen, the glib Chautauqua circuit personality, was obviously a beguiling speaker with a glittering wit; yet usually there is a discrepancy between the delightful form of decorative detail and the serious content of weighty abstraction. It is a formal sugar coating which allows the serious medicine to be taken. Often, however, the sugar mitigates against the effect of the curative. His inclination toward art, in other words, is anachronistic and undercuts the pull toward the future of his ideas. In writing about "Village Life in Norway" he describes inadvertently why the picturesque detail is so important in work such as his. "The sense of the picturesque is an entirely modern sentiment."[21] To an eighteenth century person, Norway was ugly, but as the world had become increasingly industrialized, the need for particular and colorful detail had grown. Yet Boyesen could never integrate this observation into his larger philosophy. Perhaps the missing element in his Realistic philosophy is apparent here. The Realist, if he is to preserve art, is going to have to remain close to individuals and things. To Boyesen, however, remaining close to the individual thing seemed part of a dangerous Romanticism which ignored the wave of generalization that science was introducing. Individualization of detail led to chaos. Boyesen, on the contrary, felt that we should feel the "living prototype"[22] behind characters and see the general truth which resides in all particulars.

Boyesen was attempting to hold together popular culture and
an intellectual view of the arts. He was democratic enough that
he appreciated mass education in the universities and on the
Chautauqua circuits, that he shared the new middle class's admiration of technology, that he supported the ordinary man's
pragmatism; yet he still feared the threat of Philistinism under-
mining the world of intellect. Britain's intellectual class had
failed, he maintained, because it did not separate itself from
the worshippers of Mammon and lacked the temerity to do so.[23]
Yet while critical of the alliance between intellectuals and Philistines, he could quite good-humoredly joke about the necessity
of young artists and intellectuals marrying the daughters of the
Philistines and using their ample dowries made in the sordid
marketplace to support artistic and intellectual aspirations.

His ambivalence about Philistinism is revealed in his attitude
toward the poet Swinburne. Swinburne had obviously avoided
succumbing to Philistinism, Boyesen believed, but in so doing
he separated himself from reality. He was granted the right by the
British Philistine class to "rave melodiously about a revolutionary
sunrise which he professes to espy beyond his misty horizon.
But then Swinburne is a poet for the few and can never be suf-
ficiently popular to be dangerous. Even his complicated can-
zonettes or ballades or villanelles about babies' shoes and
stockings appeal chiefly to those who are unacquainted with these
articles in the original."[24]

A Philistine, it would appear Boyesen believed, is more likely
to be familiar with the "articles in the original" than a poet. The
poetic sentiment, as Boyesen explained, belonged more to the
martial spirit—that is, it belonged to anachronistic institutions
of which Boyesen disapproved more strongly than he did Philistinism. Philistines were of the class of people whom he satirized,
but they were also the people he lived with and knew. He
married a person out of that class and almost always wrote about
them. In writing literary criticism for journals directed to people
of the Philistine class, he freely admitted that such criticism was
tied to the interests of the world of business, indicating the dependent relationship between publishers and journals. He appreciated work which from a publisher's standpoint was saleable
because "it appeals to the average reader."[25] He joined with

nineteenth century publishers in speculating about the end of poetry, for reasons it appears may have been Philistine or may have been part of his overall theory of literature. "A very intelligent friend of mine insists that poetry is an obsolescent art and that the democracy of the future will entirely dispense with it. Likewise he sees in the decorative purposes to which the arts are now being applied, an evidence that they will merely retain their places as trades of a higher degree, ministering to the material comfort of those who can afford to invest in superior skill."[26] Art would be merely some sort of superior technology which belongs to those rich enough to afford it. Art then, it appears, would belong to the Philistines.

Yet Boyesen also believed that we are evolving away from artistic beauty as we have known it, because we are moving toward an appreciation of a new unknown type of beauty which will be more intellectual and less emotional than that which the nineteenth century celebrated. The new beauty would be far removed from the gingerbread decoration of Philistine houses. Boyesen's own art seemed to be moving toward the elimination of the necessity of art. Evolution, he believed, would lead finally to a state where neither art nor laws are necessary, a state where "everything becomes literature when it is done well."[27] In other words, literature will become "a sort of Olympus, where all struggles and inequalities vanish, where all reconciliations are brought about."[28]

Boyesen believed in this Olympus as finally an intellectual height at which art as we know it and law disappear. While opposed to anarchism in the present, as represented by Ibsen, he could imagine a future time when such a lawless world will be possible: "As mankind in the course of its evolution gradually drops its predatory impulses, the laws which now are needed to keep these impulses under restraint will become superfluous."[29]

Boyesen, then, if he could have lived long enough, might have overcome his sinful yearning for the picturesque detail, even as decoration, and would have concentrated instead on the prototype. As society evolved upward to one high level, Boyesen believed, the prototype would become self-apparent. Then life would be art and art would be life, and his novels and those of others which teach reality would become unnecessary.

CHAPTER 7

The Major Phase

DURING the last five years of his life, Boyesen's talent and theory coalesced. He was ready to create novels which had the complexity necessary to make them vital and the intellectual authority to command respect. Boyesen had wanted to write a novel which was a *Kulturroman*, the quality he had appreciated in George Washington Cable's *The Grandissimes*.[1] Now that he had a well-developed evolutionary overview of American culture, he was able to identify the larger forces which contended in the struggle for survival. But he also had enough novelistic flair to give characters in this struggle individual identities, and he had enough sense of form to draw a large, multifaceted, yet unifed battlefield.

I The Mammon of Unrighteousness

The Mammon of Unrighteousness (1891) is the story of the family of the president of an upstate New York college which strongly resembles Cornell University. President Larkin's children, two brothers, Horace and Aleck, and an adopted daughter, Gertrude, are at that stage in life where they are deciding on marriages and careers. Horace Larkin is coldly calculating, both in setting up a legal and political career and in his choice of the wealthy, aristocratic Kate Van Schaak for his wife. Aleck Larkin, on the contrary, is idealistically seeking meaning in his life. He joins his brother in the practice of law, but when he discovers that his law partner brother is using the firm to advance his own political ambitions, Aleck resigns from the firm and goes to New York to establish himself as a writer, an untainted profession. Gertrude is also interested in being an artist (she sculpts), and she similarly seeks the meaningful life. Early in the novel, she

128

accepts a marriage proposal from a romantic intellectual phony named Dr. Hawk, a man who is interested in Gertrude for her adoptive family's money. To discover her life's purpose, she has to break her mistaken engagement and rebel against her authoritarian adoptive father. She does so by taking a forbidden trip to New York to help her ne'er do well real mother. The real mother, a narcotics addict, however, is undeserving of her help, and Gertrude finds herself in the city unable to return home and with no place to go. At this point, Aleck comes to her rescue, an act which ultimately leads to marriage. Once married the couple, who had formerly lived as brother and sister, must struggle to achieve a happy domestic life. While Gertrude and Aleck eventually find happiness, Kate and Horace become increasingly miserable. Kate tries to buy a diplomatic position for her husband and in numerous other ways encourages him to sell out to achieve political advancement. Thus, a kind of poetic justice is worked out in the course of the novel in which Horace suffers for his moral failings while Gertrude and Aleck prosper.

The Mammon of Unrighteousness is Boyesen's best and most Realistic work of art. It is Realistic in its avoidance of a sentimentalization of women of wealth and fashion, in its development of characters who are living individuals rather than just recognizable types, and in its attempt to document many aspects of American life—the small town, the university, politics, and the world of fashion. Each subject here is treated with greater specificity than before. For example, the world of fashion is not merely that of the rich, but that of family as well. Boyesen extends his criticism of Philistinism to include an indictment of America's propensity to create a sham aristocracy which, in imitation of European feudalism, is inimical to American democratic vitality. Indeed, Boyesen seems to appreciate the vulgar Philistine whose energy creates wealth, while he has nothing but scorn for the man who with inherited wealth and name does nothing in life but copy slavishly the lifestyle of Europeans. The novel is also Realistic in its wedding of form and content. Although as before ideas sometimes appear superimposed upon a conventional plot in order to make it meaningful, here, as in Howells' *A Hazard of New Fortunes*, often ideas expressed are a natural extension of characterization. The ideas do not identify

character with a stereotype as did those of Delia Saunders or
Ruth Copely, but instead are connected with the dynamic conflicts within characters. For example, Horace Larkin's notions
about evolution and the survival of the fittest are not merely
concepts to be considered in relation to other concepts; they
represent his attempt toward self-realization, and in the end,
they represent his mistake, for strong as he was, he is a loser in
life because of his very devotion to brute strength. Real victory
in life, as Aleck Larkin demonstrates, comes from internal
strength, the ability to know what you need to do for moral and
spiritual survival and the ability to do it.

Alternatives such as these are rather portentously suggested
in the unpromising opening chapter.

"I mean to be true to myself—true to my convictions," ejaculated
Alexander Larkin, impetuously, and the echo flung back the words
with the same impetuousity from the rock opposite.
"I mean to succeed," said Horace, his brother, and the echo immediately asserted, with the same positiveness, that it meant to succeed.[2]

With such a beginning, one might expect the novel to continue
with the ponderous didacticism of some of Boyesen's earlier
fiction. However, we come to see that all right is not with
Alexander and all evil not with Horace. Although the novel metes
out poetic justice in the end, as Alexander, after years of priva-
tion, acquires the material success he supposedly rejected and
moves into the Larkin family mansion, the novel does not naively
presuppose that right moral principles always lead to happiness.
Alexander and Gertrude's married life is presented as a series of
minor conflicts. Scenes of marital bliss alternate with quarrels
which, while never serious, are often at the verge of seriousness.
At the same time, Horace Larkin's miserable marriage does serve
a positive purpose; it encourages a kind of moral reawakening on
his part. Once, after having been crushed in an argument with
his calculating, aristocratic wife, he returned to the legislature,
filled with a kind of moral outrage, and spoke courageously
against political chicanery.

Yet Horace's moral outrage is not the product of rational de-
liberation; it is instinctual, and one might note that Horace

immediately retrenches himself afterwards, fearing that an alliance with those politicians attracted to him because of his morality might be impractical. This whole matter of instinct, the way in which it prompts a man to do what is right, raises the question of just how Realistic this novel is. The debate between two rational alternatives presented so clearly at the opening of the novel becomes instead a contest between rational and irrational factors, with man's irrational goodness taking precedence. When calculation returns after Horace's momentary lapse from reason, his wife is there to point out that a moral stance carefully taken can create power for a man. Such moral stances, of course, have nothing to do with fixed moral principles. In his picture of the political scene, Boyesen demonstrates that real morality has little to do with such political positions as that of the Republicans against the former slaveholding states.

The way in which Boyesen brings up the matter of instinct and pits it against calculation makes him seem either Romantic or Naturalistic. In a sense Boyesen is here critical of a type of realism separate from but akin to literary Realism. This is the realism of the marketplace and the high society parlor, the realism by which society dames and businessmen lead their lives. Here not only is philosophical idealism rejected as irrelevant to people whose lives are ruled by pragmatism, but all moral standards must also fall by the way. Morality, in this light, is unrealistic, even sentimental. Horace represents such an unsentimental view of man; he is a creature in a vicious struggle for survival. Horace says with some conviction, "we imagine that instincts and passions have been given us for our own personal happiness and gratification, when all the while they subserve only some general purpose, such as the preservation of the race and the welfare of society" (166). Survival of the type is what is important, and such survival is best guaranteed by each man's struggling, without external restraint, for his own success. Such a view of life is prosaic, one which nearly denies the value of art itself. As a method of art, Realism attempted disinterestedness and a similarly unromantic view of reality. It seems that the next logical step for Realism would have been to find moral standards themselves too Romantic for literature. Instead, we find Howells clinging tenaciously to an individualism which valued the survival of soul and conscience. In his world, in which fixed moral standards were failing, man must work out his individual salvation against the machinations of society. Boyesen seemed to believe in the moral necessity of man's selecting the solution which benefits the race and not just the individual.

In *The Mammon of Unrighteousness* Boyesen often demonstrates that the instinctive response to experience is the warmly human one, while the rational response is coldly mechanical. Horace's legislative speech is a good example of impulsive goodness. In addition, Alexander's severing himself from his brother's law firm when he discovers that the firm is being used to advance Horace politically, and Gertrude's breaking off her relationship with the false romantic Dr. Hawk and her trip to New York against her father's wishes to give aid to her drug-addicted mother, are examples of actions taken on impulse for moral reasons. Yet Boyesen's view of moral action is hardly simplistic, for none of these impulsive actions is done from totally pure motives, and none is successful in accomplishing its stated moral objective. Alexander's departure from his brother's firm ironically allows his brother to be corrupt without restraint. Moreover, Alexander's departure is self-serving; he always wanted to be a writer rather than a lawyer. Similarly, Gertrude does not leave home solely out of compassion for her mother's plight. She is asserting her own individualism by rebelling against her father. In addition, her decision to go to New York is sadly mistaken. Her mother had lied to her, attaching herself parasitically to her daughter's compassion. Gertrude, as her father knew, could do nothing to save her mother, neither with love or money. Thus we find the richness of the novel, for moral dilemmas are well defined, and interestingly, there are no right answers, just as there are no heroic figures who are capable of transcendent virtue. Good instincts seem superior to calculation, but instincts themselves, representing both man's animalistic and spiritual desire to survive, are complex, both good and evil.

What makes the novel an artistic success is that the very form of the novel, a kind of self-questioning Realism, reinforces its thematic element. As a Realistic work, the novel is curiously anti-Realistic. Although the most sympathetic character, Alexander, is an aspiring Realistic writer who learns from Edmund

Clarence Stedman that prose fiction is more appropriate to his era than is poetry, Boyesen obviously does not enthusiastically take up the banner of prose. In Alexander, as in early Howells, there is a kind of irrepressible optimism which concentrates on the smiling aspects of life. Boyesen's most misled character, Horace, is like Alexander in being committed to prose; in his case, however, it is in life rather than in art, and such prose is on the side opposite to ideals. Alexander says to Horace, " 'You have no poetry in you, no ideals.' " To which Horace replies, " 'You could not pay me a greater compliment. Life's substance is prose, and thus it is prose I wish to master' " (7).

Yet Horace discovers later how dangerous to a man's happiness this prose is. After Horace celebrates his wife's beauty in an internal reverie, she turns on him with cold cruel words. He thinks: "For she was his, this ominously beautiful and formidable piece of womanhood, this complex and superior creature for whom so many had sued in vain" (313). But when in helping her remove her cloak he accidentally snags her hair with his collar button, she snaps: "Oh, what a clumsy baboon you are" (314). Horace, of course, should have known that this is what he had asked for: "He had exalted the prose of life and scouted its poetry; and life had taken him at his word. For this was prose with a vengeance" (311).

Kate Van Schaak, the prosaic woman who becomes Horace's wife, may be a stereotype, just as so many women before in Boyesen's fiction were stereotypes, but this time the lack of definition itself seems part of her character. The omniscient narrator seldom goes into Kate's mind. Occasionally, we are allowed to see enough of her thinking to understand just why a New York City socialite would want to marry a rural upstate New York politician. Her reason is that she views the scheming and climbing of business and politics as being essentially similar to the machinations necessary if one were to hold one's place in society. Desiring to escape the vulgarities of American society, she sees in Horace an opportunity to flee to Europe. She merely has to mitigate his American angularity. He will contribute the political renown while she will contribute the money (without his knowledge) requisite to an important diplomatic appointment. Most of the time, however, we see only her exterior, which is a stereotype of the cold society matriarch Boyesen had presented before. Development of a personality, however, would be inconsistent in Kate's characterization, for she is so committed to fashion, to things being *comme il faut*, that having an individual identity would be a kind of romantic extravagance; it might even be vulgar.

What seems remarkable about Kate is her similarity to those heroines Boyesen had idealized before. It is almost as if Boyesen were repenting of his past sins. We may remember that Constance Douglas is a woman who comes from a good family, a girl who has aristocratic predilections, a woman who represents the pinnacle of salon society, who also is devoted to things being *comme il faut*. Although Boyesen hints that Constance Douglas might have her limitations, he never achieves a real detachment. It is implied that Julian Burroughs will be able to solve all his problems through unification with this unspecifiedly divine woman. In *The Mammon of Unrighteousness*, however, one may find characters believing in such divine reconciliations, but the author evidently does not. Both Dr. Hawk and Horace profess to be moved and inspired by the perfection of form in the women they admire. In actuality, however, their appreciation of form is merely a rationalization, covering the prosaic truth that both are marrying for money. Kate Van Schaak's great fortune is the principle source of her beauty, yet Horace, despite his supposed prosiness, was able to turn the insouciance of wealth into something nearly mystical. Upon seeing Kate's New York home with its Corots and expensive furnishings, Horace thinks, "How poor and sordid his past had been; how simple his aspirations; how crude his ideals" (281). Aspirations? Ideals? One has good reason to question what Horace means by these words.

Basically Horace is inconsistent: "He cherished in his heart a vague hostility to the exclusive aristocratic world which he was aspiring to enter, and he resented his own weakness in finding that desirable which he despised" (281). Later Boyesen has Aleck and Gertrude quarreling over whether they should buy a picture of a group of girls or one of dogs, and in retrospect it seems that Boyesen prefers their middlebrow tastes for prints of only decorative value to those high brow "ideals" which insist upon genuine Corots. Horace's awe before the lifestyle of the Van

Schaaks reveals, in addition, that he is himself capable of sentimentalism despite his commitment to the real. Emotionally he
is drawn to the pretty facade; he is too sentimental to realize
that what he so admires here will in the end destroy what he
most values, his own power.

Where Horace's "realism" makes it difficult for him to separate
truth and appearance, Gertrude's "romanticism" makes her easily
deceived. Just as Horace, a calculating lover, is able to change
Kate's bank account into an ethereal phenomenon, Gertrude is
able to misread Dr. Hawk's Byronic posturings as noble heroics.
To her Dr. Hawk is Hamlet, while to the reader Dr. Hawk is a
nefarious fool. Gertrude's misconception of reality, however,
stems from her excessive romanticism, while Horace's stems
from a commitment to a reason which exceeds reason and becomes sentimentalism. Horace is too unimaginative to see beyond
the appearance of things. Gertrude is too imaginative, reading
romance into appearances. She is fascinated by the Byronic Dr.
Hawk's lugubriousness. She convinces herself of the existence of
a fictitious woman in Europe who once tormented him: "She
came to the conclusion that there probably had been some new
development in relation to that odious woman who persisted in
loving him—in demanding a return in affection for her expendi-
ture of money" (91). All of Gertrude's conjectures concerning
Dr. Hawk's romance with a European woman who was giving
him money to keep his love are sentimental. She has learned
from novels that lovers must suffer, and she relishes such suffering. Little does she know that Dr. Hawk "had not deliberately
invented this romance; but he had allowed it to grow and take
shape about him, and he had encouraged it by mysterious hints,
and sighs, and guarded admissions. He felt now that it was so
much a part of him that he did not dare repudiate it. He had in
him a Byronic repugnance for the tame and commonplace lot,
and a taste for picturesque wickedness" (206).

Obviously both Gertrude and Dr. Hawk enjoy their suffering.
Gertrude's sculpture reveals the sort of romantic misery through
renunciation which she desires. Her subject matter for art includes aristocratic nuns locked in nunneries by their wicked
families. Such a nun would be a poetic character to Gertrude, yet
"she felt in herself a capacity both for renunciation and for

highminded rebellion against tyranny which could only find their proper expression if she were not a nun" (117).

Like Howells' Penelope Lapham, Gertrude wishes to martyr herself despite all common sense; she renounces her father, giving up all comforts of her present life and all hopes for a substantial inheritance. She asserts her independence against her father's apparent tyranny, not knowing that he is wise and benevolent in this case. From her misguided mission to New York to save her mother, she learns what all good Boyesen girls must learn. She vows "that she would never trust herself again; never set up her own will against that of her father" (265).

Bella Robbins, an early love of Horace's, is a character who is not quite as fully developed as Gertrude, but she is similarly inclined to value romance over actuality. She is the hysterical small town maiden, so desperate for marriage that she attaches all of her hope to a man whom she never should marry. There is no reason why Bella should love Horace Larkin. She does, however, merely because he is masculine, and in response, she attempts to be everything that is thought to be feminine. Horace to her is manly strength, boldly stated opinions (it does not matter what they are), and the smell of cigar smoke. When Horace cruelly tosses her aside, she is immune to the real truth, that he did so in order to marry a wealthier woman. Instead she believes that Horace has left her merely because of an insult delivered by her father. In actuality, the insult serves as an excuse for Horace to do what he has all along intended. After this, Bella demonstrates how dangerous such sentimental devotion to romance can be. Never healthy, when Horace breaks their engagement, she pines away. She blames her father and dies of a broken heart. Yet Boyesen is not unequivocal in denouncing romance. All along Bella has believed a falsehood about Horace rather than the truth: "What a pathetic romance, forsooth; and yet he was glad she had cherished it, glad that her last days had not been embittered with the anguish of spurned affection" (350).

The way in which characters serve as foils for each other is part of the unity of this novel. Obviously we are meant to compare and contrast Kate Van Schaak's coldly calculating view of marriage with Bella's instinctual one. Kate's problem with matrimony is that she has too many practical reasons for making the

choice she does. Bella's problem is that she has no practical reason for making the choice she does. Interestingly, Gertrude makes
an initial error, her engagement to Dr. Hawk, when she is free to
pick and choose. When no choice is available, fate makes the appropriate match. Aleck, and obviously the author, see this fate as
"a kind of innocent fatalism to which we are all more or less subject. . . . Aleck derived an exquisite delight from contemplating
the benevolent machinations of Providence on his behalf"(271).
Gertrude, unable to return to her father, incapable of supporting
herself, marries Alexander Larkin out of necessity. Thus Gertrude
demonstrates both the benefits and dangers of responding to our
instincts. Fortunately, she is taken under wing by a man more
rational than herself, and thereby her future survival is assured.

Alexander Larkin is a man much like Gertrude, however. Instinctual forces largely explain what he is and where he is going.
He too serves as a foil for the other major characters. Whereas
Horace is calculatingly realistic and Dr. Hawk is calculatingly
romantic, Aleck is a mixture, a human, emotional creature, yet
rational as well: "even in the midst of his agitations there was
a still small voice of reflection, which like a sober commentary,
accompanied the excited text" (95–96).

Aleck seems to represent the culmination of Boyesen's efforts
to present a hero who is credible as a man who lives in this
materialistic world, but still has a forcefulness of the Romantic
hero. What Aleck represents is a new romantic hero; no longer
in awe of Wordsworthian sublimity nor communicating directly
with God through intuition, Aleck stands as the natural man who
is both the animal of evolution and the culmination of a dynamic
universe which God had created and Herbert Spencer had demonstrated was complete. Thus the force of sex, so clearly confused
in many of Boyesen's earlier treatments of the girl, is here
joined with divine energy. "The eternal, beautiful mystery of
sex, which to a pure-minded, virginal man like Aleck was doubly
mysterious, filled him with *reverential* tenderness. . . . And yet
there was something remote and strange about her, something
divinely awe-inspiring; because she was that wonderful, inscrutable, exquisite and adorable thing—a woman. . . . She was the
last and best pinnacle of God's work; the supreme result of God's
creative intelligence" (274; emphasis added).

Aleck recognizes, however, that Gertrude is not the embodiment of an ideal. In one touching section, he tells Horace of
his wife's precious, irascible behavior during a quarrel. Thus,
if Aleck represents the culmination of Boyesen's attempts to
create a credible hero, Gertrude, whose mystery is simultaneously
chemical and spiritual, is Boyesen's first success with a heroine
since he left the fabulous meadow where Ragnhild reigned.
Gertrude, like Ragnhild, is a natural woman, but here the nature
the heroine responds to is naturalistic rather than transcendental.
Boyesen describes Gertrude in a natural setting: "She would
have rejoiced in the story of Nature's great and relentless war—
the unending battle for the poor privilege of life—which was
being waged in the rock, the soil, the water, and the air, had
she but known the language in which it is written" (130).

Despite the fact that Boyesen gently satirizes Gertrude's Romanticism (she is the sort of young lady who names her horse
Sir Walter Scott), she is a Romantic heroine. Nature is employed
in ways which are simultaneously Romantic and Naturalistic.
Thus, we find confusion between the spiritual and the physical.
For example, Gertrude, who finds herself in love with Dr. Hawk,
shivers with evident delight. Only later do we discover that the
shiver was the first symptom of typhoid fever. Such confusion
over whether a shiver is Romantic ecstasy or Naturalistic disease
is representative of her response to natural phenomenon: "But
sensitive as she was to every impression, she could not ward
off this pagan semi-absorption in Nature—this irresistible sympathy with the teeming, abundant, myriad-voiced, noon-day life
of summer—the strong eternally destroying, eternally creative
heart-beat of mother earth" (203). Gertrude both looks backward
to a primitive pagan response and forward to Naturalistic response. Her primitive response to nature is Romantic in its
"irresistible sympathy." Nature, however, is more than the sub-
lime force which inspired Wordsworth. Man has a more basic
tie than that; he is controlled by the same natural forces. Thus
we find that when Horace Larkin is threatened, his response is
unromantically primitive: "life was dealing outrageously with
him, rousing all the latent violence deposited in his soul by
barbaric ancestors" (361).

The Naturalistic sentiments in the novel are those expressed by Horace Larkin in a dinner table discussion. The sentiments closely parallel those associated with the lobster and the squid in Dreiser's *The Financier*:

"What makes a man estimable in your opinion?"

"The degree with which he understands how to adapt himself to his environment," Horace replied, promptly. . . .

"Would you say that the pickerel, who eats all the other fishes in his lake, is the most estimable fish?" the doctor put in, anxious to display his intellectual acumen.

"Yes, I would. In the conditions under which he lives he has the choice of eating or being eaten. I respect him for taking a clear view of the situation. . . . If the alternative is presented to me to be a beast of prey or a beast preyed upon, I prefer to be a beast of prey." (164–65)

Yet this naturalism, in its brutal reduction of humanity to an evolutionary struggle, is not Boyesen's. In both *The Mammon of Unrighteousness* and *The Golden Calf*, Boyesen tells the story of men who gain the world (who prove that they are fit to survive in an animal sense), yet lose their own souls.

II   The Golden Calf

The Golden Calf (1892) is an American success story which is simultaneously a failure story. Its hero, Oliver Tappan, "failed by a series of successes,"[3] when he left the New England small town of his birth to forge his destiny in the city. Ironically, however, as his fame widens and his wealth and power increase, his soul withers away.

Oliver Tappan, growing up in rural New England, is a bright, idealistic young man for whom it appears the future is one of great promise in service of mankind, Although his father does little to encourage his education, he is fortunate to have as his teacher Dr. Habicht, a German immigrant of tremendous learning who lives a simple life earning what little he needs from translations. Oliver, however, moves from his small town to an industrial city and begins to work his way up in the world. Each advancement he makes, however, costs a value to which he was formerly committed. Oliver justifies these compromises as necessary in order to survive in an animalistic struggle for existence. Finally, however, he forsakes his simple girl back home in order to marry a coldly ambitious society matron. His wife, Madeline, encourages all his worldly ambitions and discourages all his idealistic aspirations. At the conclusion of the story, Oliver is wealthy, living a valueless life as a lobbyist for corporate interests in Washington. His marriage is cold and loveless, and so he indulges himself in an innocent flirtation with a simple French girl whom he perceives as possessing all the life, naturalness, and spontaneity that his life and his wife lack.

Like the hero of *Honest John Vane*, by J. W. De Forest, Oliver Tappan succumbs to the temptations of power in Washington and thereby becomes a participant in the worldly corruption he had set out originally to correct. Like *Honest John Vane*, Boyesen's novel is heavily didactic. It does not, however, end with a sermon against the evils of the system in Washington, evils which the public might correct when they are delineated. De Forest writes from the vantage point of the optimistic liberal, the man who believes it is institutions which are corrupt and not men. Alter the institutions, and Honest John Vane will remain honest. Boyesen too believes that institutions share responsibility in corruption. For example, the fault with America appears to be "that human depravity is less restrained under our form of government" (187). Yet no government eliminates depravity which is endemic in humankind. Instead, the opportunity to further good or evil rests with the individual. Although Boyesen, perhaps to reinforce his apparent didactic purpose, falls on Christian gospel to dramatize his message ("What profiteth it a man to gain the whole world and lose his own soul"), the Christian maxim is employed to demonstrate a naturalistic proposition—that is, the man who gives up parts of himself to make himself free ironically ends with no freedom at all. The liberally educated Oliver becomes by the end of the novel "a machine. Literature and art, which once meant something to him, have long ceased to interest him" (184). Once a powerful man who made choices about the course of his life, now he is its victim: "Our actions spin a net about us, which we cannot tear asunder" (125).

Instinct and chance play their parts in this novel also, but

Boyesen makes it clear that man need not be caught in a deterministic evolutionary struggle. Man is part of evolution, but on a higher level. He has conscious power to alter the direction of evolution. Oliver Tappan, when he leaves his home town of Traversville, is committed to directing the course of evolution upward: "To stand in the foremost ranks of the battle for human progress, to spread light into the world's dark places; to combat the political and social wrongs which are inherited in our present social condition—this was the noble ambition which the Teuton kindled in Oliver's soul" (35–36). The Teuton who instructed Oliver, Dr. Habicht, who gave him his liberal education, is an idealist. He is a sort of nineteenth century dropout who has retreated to the village, where he sustains himself on translations and avoids engaging in the competitive and sordid marketplace. As an idealistic evolutionist, Dr. Habicht believes that man should be beyond the animalistic struggle for survival, that instead he should be evolving morally. He deprecates the clamor around the Golden Calf.

According to Habicht: "Dis ravenous hunger for gold, which lurks in de bottom of every American soul—dat is a plague, a blight, a deadly fungus which kills de germ of every noble endeafor . . . . pay honor to de most successful grabber, und I dell you, you will debase de human race, you reverse its upward evolution by securing de survival—de predominance of mere base craft und cunning, und de suppression of de nobler qualities upon vhich de brogress of de race depends" (32–33). Such progress comes from "de great sum of human labors for high und exalted aims vhich pushes mankind onward" (33). Oliver learns the lesson of evolution from Dr. Habicht, but seems to forget quickly that man's struggle is not one of brute force. Oliver retrogresses quickly to his animal self, that same animal self which allowed him through physique and cunning to be a leader among the boys of his village. His sad confusion, however, is understandable. After seeing New York, sensing the immensity which reduces his own self-esteem, he determines that a man must have power and money first before he can do good. What he remembers of his lesson is that winning in the struggle is important. Ironically, the energy of liberal idealism is easily transformed into the energy employed in the brute force struggle of the marketplace. This is the irony of the liberal education which, its humanistic values set aside, provides the impetus for a man to rise from being the son of a grocer to being a rich businessman. The aspirations and the belief in progress instilled in Oliver by Dr. Habicht contribute to his success in the materialistic world. Yet Oliver's lapse cannot be entirely explained by his weakness. Dr. Habicht's homilies had little efficacy to a young man of his era: Oliver "had been born in a period of religious decadence, when the old Puritanic New England was irrevocably dead, and no new form of faith had yet taken the place of that which had been discarded" (209).

Dr. Habicht himself might have offered a "new form of faith" had he not been alien, both in birth and habit, to an American way of life. Indeed, the very fact that Boyesen, a man who went to an elocutionist to rid himself of an accent, endows Habicht with a thick and unreadable dialect indicates some disapproval. Habicht's sermons are naive and tedious; his inability to recognize his own son's moral turpitude is an intellectual failing. Therefore, he cannot be thought of as an unqualified spokesman for the author.

Without a clear distinction between right and wrong, it is no wonder that Oliver becomes confused. Hence, he is like George Eliot's Lydgate, a man with high aspirations but lacking a coherent ethic, a man unable to make decisions rationally upon a foundation of belief. Oliver, in his move from the New England village to the industrial city, is caught between the professed American belief in simple Christian values and the reality of a nation committed to plunder. Against Dr. Habicht's notions of "the ideal" and "imagination," Oliver's publisher-employer, Mr. Carter, offers different definitions. Speaking of a man worth eighteen million dollars, he says, "Such a fortune appeals mightily to the American imagination." A man with that amount of money "realizes the popular ideal" (110). In an environment where morality is defined so loosely, the Christian church is perverted; no longer representing sacred values, it is subservient to an amoral business world. For example, scripture is commonly misread in a manner which makes Christianity an instrument of capitalism. When a notoriously unethical businessman is nominated for a lay leadership position in the church—a position the scoundrel desires greatly because it will help him disguise his true character and thereby allow him greater freedom for his nefarious activities—he is defended in the following fashion: "The Gospel teaches us to be wily as serpents and harmless as doves, and if Mr. Slosson has taken the former part of this injunction more to heart than the latter, it is only because in a world as bad as this is, self preservation demands it" (60).

Women, who are removed from the vicious marketplace struggle, might be expected to have a superior, more Christian set of values which can mitigate the evil done by their husbands. Victorian culture, which often idealized the woman, assigned her the task of redeeming society. But in Boyesen's novels of social Realism, the viciousness of the social struggle causes ladies to lose track of ideals also. Whereas men seek economic self-preservation, women seek social self-preservation. While money is the gauge of a man's success, women are at one remove from money, dependent upon it, but pretending obliviousness to it. Their gauge of success measures manners and style. The cash values upon which a lady's husband's world might turn are not held to be immoral, but merely vulgar. Madeline Carter is representative of the society woman's attitude toward morality: "Moral delinquencies she held to be of small consequence, as long as they did not interfere with the delinquent's social status, but breaches of etiquette she held to be unpardonable" (81).

Thus it is no wonder that a young man whose instinct to succeed is great finds the moral pitfalls of the city unavoidable. Boyesen's vividly realistic descriptions of New York City emphasize the frightening vastness of this new world. After having been a leader in his village, Oliver is lost in the city: "Few will comprehend what torture there was to him in this thought of the cheapness of human life, which continually oppressed him in the midst of the multitude thronging the streets of the huge city" (49). The city dislocates Oliver. Mr. Carter argues with some efficacy for him that: "A man could not afford to set up a higher standard of morals than the majority of his fellow citizens . . . because if he did, he would simply get left in the race and be trampled down in the fierce struggle for existence" (77). In addition, like Horace Larkin upon seeing the splendor which wealth can create, the small town boy changes his idea of what

144   htl;dr

constitutes virtue. The shoddiness of his past life seems sordid, while the glamor of New York seems virtuous. The style of society replaces ethics; all unpleasantness and moral inadequacy are gilded over. Upon seeing the riches of the Carter home, "insensibly, his view of life was changed; and his imagination conjured up pictures of the future, far more resplendent than those which had formerly satisfied his ambition" (54).

In a sense, the novel is a criticism of both prose and Realism as they are popularly conceived. As in *The Mammon of Unrighteousness*, what is good in the hero is romantic, impulsive, and poetic. Like a Bogart hero, Oliver (and Horace Larkin as well), is cynical, but has a sentimental instinct for good underneath. Unfortunately, such good instincts do not insure good actions. A good system is needed to reinforce man's natural goodness and to repress his natural evil. In the world of *The Golden Calf*, however, no system—not even as a value structure—exists. Hence Oliver is confused. Hearing so often of the "popular ideal" of the city, he forgets the hazy anachronistic values of the small town. Language of the old values is arbitrarily applied to the new corruption in an attempt to justify it. Hence the reader learns that a lobbyist for railroad interests in Washington must be "a man of high principles and good morals," when it is obvious that what is required is a facade of decency in order to mitigate the actuality of his evil work (76). Such "high principles," distorted as they are, become in the "reality" of New York a justification for compromised lives. Besides, it is easy to discredit the goodness of those in Traversville. Minna, the instinctively good Wordsworthian primitive back home, does not face the challenges Oliver does: "It was so much easier to be good in Traversville than in New York; and it was not to be denied that the citadel of a woman's integrity was rarely subject to such fierce assaults as was that of man" (210-11).[4]

Romantic primitives who live in the country are removed from the struggle in which city men must be engaged. Defensively, Oliver assumes that failure in the present corrupt system has nothing to do with moral superiority, but only with weakness, the inability to win. In the world of animalistic evolution, one must respond to the challenge to fight or else he is deemed unfit:

"I suppose lack of success argues greatness with you," Oliver rejoined, piqued at the implied reproach, "just as prosperity and a readiness to take advantage of the chances that come in your way argue sordidness of purpose and surrender to Mammon. I know that every impecunious ne'er-do-well is apt to console himself with the notion that he is too good for this world, or the world is too bad for him. But I have no patience with such pitiful self-delusion. If a man doesn't get on, it is because of some defect in his character or his ability—because there is a screw loose somewhere in his mental machinery." (69–70)

Oliver's case is well argued and is not entirely in error, just as Dr. Habicht is not entirely right. The closing image of the passage above is telling. In order to eliminate such defects of character which cause one to malfunction, one must adjust his mental "machinery." He cannot even have an individualizing loose screw. Oliver learns "How civilization, so-called, does stamp all individuality out of our souls and reduces us all, for good or for ill, to mere industrial or commercial or social machines, each of which is so like all the rest that we might, just as well, for purpose of identification be numbered as named" (162).

Hence, despite Boyesen's condemnation of Romantic individualism, the Romantic instinct appears to be all that keeps man from being a number. In the midst of Oliver's "real" new world, occasionally an impulse of good arises and he finds that he must depend upon his "rational" self to check his quixotic nature. Offered the opportunity to lobby for the railroads, his first impulse is to reject indignantly "the assault upon his honor" (77). When he proposes to Madeline and tells her of his past engagement, uncontrolled emotion, sacred love as opposed to his profane love of the rich girl, arises in him at the mention of Minna's name. Society, as it has stamped out individuality, has also repressed his emotional instincts. Unlike Bogart, he does not show his true warmheartedness in the end. Instead, involved in an innocent flirtation with a French girl, Oliver sees how far he is from natural instinctive life: "What a yawning chasm separated the type of womanhood which Juanita represented from that of his prim, frigid, anaemic wife, whose slim, flat bosom had never been invaded by a lawless impulse, a generous desire, or a strong and noble aspiration" (162).

What makes *The Golden Calf* seem Naturalistic is that Oliver, strongest and best-educated of the boys of the village, fails while doing that which is most natural for an American boy. Retreating to a Walden is a possibility of which Boyesen would not dream. Oliver seeks "Activity—exciting, ambitious, fiercely engrossing activity" (135). The city is a natural arena for such activity, for it is not only Babylon, but an enchanting, lively place which naturally draws young men to it. Boyesen at times lauds the city with the indiscriminateness of the vitalist: "There was something splendid and imposing in the mere vastness of the great city, with its myriad human lives, its seething activities, its beauty and its ugliness, its wealth and its misery" (205).

The Golden Calf is Boyesen's most pessimistic novel. A young man does what his energy compels him to do and thereby loses his natural goodness, his soul, his humanity, and his individuality. His downward moral journey is by small steps. Minor moral weaknesses lead later to major moral catastrophes. He loses not because he made one conscious error, but because, as an all-American boy, he does not have as much moral strength as he has energy. Like Clyde in Dreiser's *An American Tragedy*, his choices seem made for him by accidents. For example, even his proposal to Madeline is not meant to be such, but is the consequence of a misunderstanding. Although cosmic law does not destroy Oliver, as it might the protagonist of a Naturalistic novel, it is clear that humanistic values stand little chance in this society. Oliver is caught in a void. The Puritan values of the small town can not sustain him in a city where men, like animals, thwart the noble direction of evolution.

III Social Strugglers

Social Strugglers (1893), Boyesen's last major work, also represents the void of values in the American big city. When a newly rich family moves to the East, the father abdicates his role as leader, allowing the mother to carry on an unscrupulous battle in the social war. The simple Philistine vitality of the small town businessman is evidently preferable to the effete pseudoaristocracy of the city, but small town patriarchy stands no chance pitted against the wicked New York matriarchy.

After earning millions, Peleg Lemmuel Bulkley, at the insistence of his powerful wife, sells his tailoring concern in the Midwest, and takes his family and his millions to New York in order that his wife and his three daughters may advance themselves socially. New York, they find, is cold to them. The faces of the fashionable which they pass on Fifth Avenue look through the well-dressed Bulkley women without seeing them. It takes a happy accident to open the door to society a crack. One afternoon in the theater, Maud Bulkley and her sister, Peggy, are in a box which they share with two gentlemen strangers. Maud cannot help but overhear the conversation between the young men, and she learns that one has a home at Atterbury which he may rent out for the summer. Coincidentally, the socially rejected Bulkleys have been seeking a summer residence, but fear the formidable society of Newport. The overheard conversation in combination with the stunning effect that two such dandies have upon Maud is further impressed upon her memory by an act of minor heroism which is performed by one of them. As the audience is leaving the theater, a thief grabs her expensive umbrella. Philip Warburton apprehends the villain and returns the umbrella to her.

The accidental encounter leads ultimately to the Bulkleys (who now call themselves the P. Leamington Bulkleys at Mrs. Bulkley's insistence) renting the home of the other gentleman in the theater box, a Mr. Fanchley. Fanchley, a foil to Warburton, is a man who has been irresponsible with his wealth. Instead of being a noble man rescuing the Bulkleys from their plight, he is a nearly ruined landowner who rents his summer home to them to cover present debts. Despite his precarious financial circumstances, Fanchley is convinced of his social value. If it were not for his debts, he would never rent to such vulgar people. The blue bloods of Atterbury prefer to ignore the Bulkleys until another accident makes them unignorable. By fluke, a controlling share of Atterbury's exclusive Beach Club is placed in P. L. Bulkley's hands. Under the customary direction of his wife, Bulkley uses his stock as a lever to get them invited to join the club. Once in the club, little attention is paid to them until one day by chance Warburton sees the female Bulkleys walking by themselves about the club grounds. Remembering the two

Bulkley daughters and taking pity on them, he decides to help
them by making a few crucial introductions.

Maud Bulkley finds herself poised between the ludicrous social
climbing of her mother and a desire for something more meaningful. Warburton becomes her suitor, but is forced to leave
Atterbury before she can make any commitment to either him
or his superior values. In addition, Warburton suffers financial
reversals which he, unlike Fanchley, makes no attempt to hide.
As a consequence of Warburton's misfortune, Maud turns her
head to the flattering attention of the real ne'er do well, Fanchley.
When Fanchley proposes, Maud knows she should not accept,
but the moment overtakes her: he offers too much in the way of
social advantage for her and her family for Maud to refuse.
Meanwhile, Warburton suffers the loss of Maud to his friend;
the loss of his father first to the disgrace of bankruptcy and then
death; and subsequently, the loss of all his own wealth in order
to honor his father's debts, something honesty rather than law
has compelled him to do. After sustaining these losses, Warburton
turns his back on society, involving himself in a selfless mission
to the poor. Warburton and Maud are not reunited until near
the end of the novel when Maud and a group of fashionable
friends go slumming in a ghetto filled with recent arrivals from
Italy and Poland. When some of the poor react violently to the
apparent disinterest of these elegant ladies, the voyeurs are
forced to seek refuge in a mission which just happens to be the
one in which Warburton works. Maud's final conversion from the
shallow values of society to real social concern, the climax of
the book, takes place here. The episode points to the final scene
of the novel, in which Warburton articulates his social program
and, incidentally, proposes.

The hero, Philip Warburton, despite his lifelong ties with New
York aristocracy, is strangely untainted. Unlike the ineffectual
goodness of Alexander Larkin and Dr. Habicht, he has a strength
which they lack. Although Larkin and Habicht remain pure and
uncompromised, they are, nevertheless, peripheral to society.
They escape corruption by being true to themselves, but their
lives make little difference to the larger society. Warburton,
however, not only escapes corruption, but becomes an active
agent to fight against the inequities of his society. He is a Chris-

tian social worker fighting his nineteenth century war on poverty in the slums of Manhattan. With such a hero, *Social Strugglers* is much more of a propaganda novel than any Boyesen had written before. In earlier works Boyesen has men who escape the corruption of a Philistine world by becoming writers. The writers, of course, can indirectly contribute to reform by supplying the education which is prerequisite to an altered society. Warburton, however, while not by any means a revolutionary, is an active reformer, attempting to effect change. As such, he becomes the spokesman for his vision of a utopian world. Since his speeches often interfere with the romantic plot of the novel, and since he is a static character, consistently good from beginning to end, he is less the Realistic hero than those of other late Boyesen novels. Obviously Boyesen intended greater didacticism than in *A Golden Calf* or *The Mammon of Unrighteousness*. While Habicht is easily discredited and Alexander Larkin is not always strong, Warburton is represented as Boyesen's example of the successful man who aids in this romantic evolutionary struggle, contributing to the survival of the morally fittest.

The novel, however, combines Romanticism in the form of this idealized hero with a kind of Naturalism in the story of the Bulkley family. In the quasi-Naturalistic world of *A Golden Calf*, no forces remained to save the noble boy from moral ruin. In this novel, the Bulkleys are similarly alone in their struggle to survive in New York society. Boyesen describes the dehumanization by the city in Naturalistic ways: "It is a most curious feeling which possesses a person living in the midst of a vast and populous community which takes no notice of him—to which he is a mere undistinguished human atom—an animated agglomeration of dust labelled for the sake of convenience with a name. The feeling is perhaps proximately one of reckless irresponsibility and the consequent temptation to throw duty, propriety and all restraints to the winds."[5]

The story of Maud Bulkley, how she is almost ruined by circumstances and how she is saved, is simultaneously the most Naturalistic and the most Romantic aspect of the novel. Maud's life appears to be run by chance; the laws of the universe seem reflected in the deterministic struggle of New York society where simple innocence does not stand a chance. What Maud Bulkley

learns, the readers are supposed to learn. She moves from her
father's selfish disinterest in things social, to an interest in
fashionable society which at one point is so strong that she becomes engaged to a prominent man she does not love, and
finally to an interest in Warburton's type of social values. The
move is one from a shallow understanding of her world based
on Romantic literature, to a ruthless but supposedly realistic
social climbing, to, finally, a deep recognition that life offers
richer meaning to those who are true to themselves alone. Hence,
one sees in this novel, as has been seen before in Boyesen, a rejection of shallow sentimental Romanticism, as well as a rejection
of the materialism of the marketplace. The Naturalistic laws of
evolution provide for Boyesen a new mystery, a new hierarchy
in which men will reach the ideal by climbing the evolutionary
ladder. His view would be deterministic if science were not
leading to that new mystery. The predetermined direction of
man's evolution is paradoxically toward greater freedom and
humanity: evolution does not reduce men to animals, but uplifts
them to the gods.

Social Strugglers is a complex novel which can be compared
to Howells' *The Rise of Silas Lapham* as well as his *A Hazard
of New Fortunes*. The ambiguity of the title indicates its complexity, because the book is about social climbers, about those
who must struggle merely to survive, and about those who
struggle to change society. In the novel, two significant factors
determine action. First are the accidents which bring about
whatever real social advances are made. Accidents indicate simultaneously the willy-nilly makeup of society and the coincidental
quality of individual experience, which forces one to seize the
moment if he is to realize himself in moral terms. Second is the
force of matriarchy. It is a woman, Mrs. Bulkley, who operates
as the most significant force in the social world of the Bulkley
family. In this vacuum of values, women rule. She determines
that the Bulkleys must forsake the Baptist church for Anglican-
ism, the West for New York, and their real name for one which
sounds aristocratic. She also makes up a family coat of arms, is
influential in Maud's acceptance of a proposal from a man she
does not love, and then, at the conclusion of the novel, joins the
society of other grande dames who rule the fashionable world.

Her strength is opposed to the masculine unassuming Christianity of Philip Warburton, which demonstrates itself in several heroic acts. As in *The Rise of Silas Lapham*, society is dominated by women, but the influence here is not the benign influence of Mrs. Lapham, who represents the good Christian ladies who rule the small towns. In this novel it is the women who have forsaken the old values—church ties become social connections; manners replace morals; all is subsumed in the battle for status.

Against the cruel world of chance and matriarchy there is the gentle world of the social worker Warburton. When his ideology gets inserted even into the culminating proposal scene, however, one cannot help but feel that the novel falters as a work of art. The novel of manners becomes too explicitly a propaganda novel. The motivating interest of romance, one which must have carried many a nineteenth century young lady ecstatically from page to page, is overwhelmed at the end by the message. Boyesen does not want the reader to be confused, so he makes it clear that the love of Philip and Maud is not physical; it is Platonic. In addition, Warburton, who is never entirely credible, loses what little remains of his humanity when he takes up the cause. The synthesis between idea and sentiment which the book had achieved earlier is lost.

Yet overall Warburton represents well the type of man who might save society. In Boyesen's three great novels of the 1890s he seemed mystified with the energy of this increasingly wealthy society. In factories and in fashionable parlors, a struggle was going on. The victors liked to dignify their achievement, calling it the survival of the fittest. But Boyesen knew better and hoped instead that out of all this conflict there would result a moral evolution toward a better society. While many in society sought money and status, a few were untainted by this sordid struggle. For the corrupt, the lesson the nineteenth century taught was to be hard headed if you were a man or cold hearted if you were a woman, rationalizing that this was necessary if one were to be realistic. Boyesen aspired, however, to a higher sort of realism. Success at such a price, Boyesen demonstrated, brought its concomitant miseries. To Boyesen it was better to act on instincts and with a warm heart. Of course, we must realistically balance sentiment with practicalities; moral success required a synthesis of emotion and realism. Yet the hope was that if individuals could achieve such a reconciliation, society could as well. Such syntheses would carry society upward in evolutionary progress. Hence Aleck realistically abjures the mammon of uprighteousness, and Oliver Tappan learns, albeit too late, that he does not want the golden calf. Such a lesson is not too late for the reader, however. If in life we must be social strugglers, Boyesen seemed to say, let us know what the real struggle, the moral struggle, is about, and let us lead men and women into the better world which is to come. This is what Warburton does. Boyesen ends his career as a novelist representing, realistically, he believes, the man who is both effective and good.

CHAPTER 8

Conclusion

I *Boyesen's Place in Intellectual History*

THE irony of Realism is often subtle and can be explained partially on the basis of the Realists' association with pragmatic philosophy. Instead of being simply monistic materialists, as many of their later brethren of the Naturalist school were to become, the Realists were often pluralistic. To William James' way of thinking: "If 'materialism' means the unintelligibility and uncontrollability of nature, then pragmatism means the opposite. But if 'materialism' means the belief that mind is made of the same stuff as matter, is subject to the same ultimate laws, and therefore is able truly to know matter, then pragmatism agrees."[1]

William James, who asked the question "Does Consciousness Exist?," was complemented in his exploration of the relation of mind to matter by the work of his brother Henry. Henry James used irony to increase our sense of complexity in humans. When Isabel Archer confronts her destiny or Christopher Newman learns that he may have been a guileless fool, one sees the difficulty of mind meeting and understanding experience. Yet men can be, after all, finely tuned sensibilities, able to recognize when one is behaving badly. They may suffer setbacks, but knowledge of principles seems possible; a center of consciousness may never understand these principles, but the implied author can indicate that they definitely exist without designating what they are.

Howells' irony is somewhat simpler, but is based on the same type of materialism which assumes general principles. Often Howells will just photograph a situation for us to interpret. In his novels of manners, for example *The Rise of Silas Lapham*, one sees an objectively photographed situation where characters have conflicting ways of viewing the same social events. The

153

Corey dinner party is representative. Material, after all, can be truthfully treated. If man looks at experience hard enough, he will understand it.

Stephen Crane's impressionistic style implies epistemological skepticism. While the implied author stands behind Henry Fleming, counterpointing his assertion that "He was a man" with an ironic tone, he nevertheless indicates in descriptions of landscapes—some of them described from a vantage point other than Henry's consciousness—that no sensate knowledge is complete. All men are beguiled by the appearances of things. The accidents of light and shade make reality unknowable. Thus, Crane's irony is very complex, for Henry Fleming and the author of *The Red Badge of Courage* are at varying distances from each other. Crane has moved away from pragmatism, presenting matter in part as uncontrollable and unknowable; yet his dependence on an ironic contrast between differing levels of certainty indicates that pragmatism informs his thinking.

Boyesen's irony, however, is not epistemological. It does not stem from discordant views of reality. Instead, Boyesen works from an absolute standard which is not subject to the same laws as matter. Boyesen's evolutionary theory assumes a unity which exists independently of material demonstration. While James' and Howells' standards come from matter itself, Boyesen's grow from idealistic principles. In the manner of an Augustan, one sure of his absolute standards and values, Boyesen engages in satirical reduction of characters. The irony is verbal and its purpose seems always to be to make people simple, to reduce material complexity in the face of the omniscient author's intellectual certainty.

Irony in Boyesen's novels of manners is satirical in the eighteenth century sense, rather than the painful, although still comic, irony of isolated men in the psychological novel of manners. Boyesen could never really get involved in the whole problem of self-knowledge which is basic to Silas Lapham, Henry Fleming, and Christopher Newman. Either he was not enough of an innovative ironist to represent such problems, or his view of reality was too simplistic to recognize the great difficulties involved in man's knowing experience.

Einar Falconberg knows who he is; his problem is making it

public. Julian Burroughs, like a Jamesian character, does not know who he is, but he lacks the central viable core that makes Christopher Newman, Isabel Archer, and Lambert Strether palpable human beings despite their vicissitudes. The reductive irony Boyesen uses cannot allow us the dual sense of a character as both strong and weak that James' center of consciousness does. James allows us to see that a strong mind when wrong is nevertheless strong. Boyesen's irony reduces characters to stereotypes. He punctures their pretensions of romantic grandeur, but the irony used seems often that of a sophomoric mind which thrusts satiric barbs at people it is not the least bit interested in understanding.

This irony creates the sociological quality of Boyesen's fiction, for characters are reduced to representative types. It also contributes to the unfortunate didacticism. Boyesen belongs with those writers who stand on one side of a dichotomy between imaginative writing and a variety of political writing. Boyesen often failed to place himself imaginatively inside the consciousness of characters he viewed ironically. He tried with Gertrude and with Oliver Tappan of *A Golden Calf*, but technically he was unable. His type of irony destroys empathy. Let us imagine for a moment what James would have done with the story of a man such as Oliver, who failed by a series of successes. For Boyesen it was largely a reworking of the Judas-Faust betrayal story. It becomes Jamesian in that the hero seems not to understand what is happening until it is too late. He is, after all, but an impressionable farm boy in an impressionistic world. How was he to see the corruption under the big city glitter? Boyesen neglects the irony of impressionism to emphasize his moral, "What doth it profit a man to gain the whole world and lose his own soul?" The question, Boyesen assumes, is rhetorical. For James it would not be so, for he would proceed to answer the question, not unequivocally. The fortunate fall into knowledge which characterizes so many modern novels was not part of Boyesen's psychology or theology.

The division I have made above between imaginative writing and political writing is similar to Parrington's distinction between sociological and psychological fiction. Their separation is an unnecessary one. The moral and political truths of fiction do not come in spurts of bombast, which make the other side impossible to imagine; it is the imaginative leap into an opposing viewpoint, James' capacity to become Newman, that gives a book moral and even political relevance.

This political, sociological, didactic element, which Boyesen expresses through the use of satirical irony, associates him more with the Genteel Tradition than with international, ideological literary movements such as Realism or Naturalism. Boyesen's friends, Edmund Clarence Stedman and Thomas Bailey Aldrich, were from that circle. Derived from American Puritanism and more allied with authoritarian humanism than with individualistic American democracy, the Genteel Tradition has qualities relevant to Boyesen. "While this gentility was developing, the meaning of words was changing and narrowing. For instance, 'Puritanism' was slowly coming to mean an exclusive, moral traditionalism and 'humanism' was coming to mean an equally exclusive cultural traditionalism."[2]

Boyesen's voice is often that of moral traditionalism, and his European-Nordic sense of culture gives him the added tone of exclusive cultural traditionalism. Yet it is not accurate to deprecate Boyesen because of certain similarities to a literary circle in general disrepute. Boyesen, like Howells, cannot be identified purely with the Genteel Tradition. True, Howells shared with this group an aversion to topics shocking to young ladies, but both Howells and Boyesen shared qualities which make them quite ungenteel. Both were too democratic, too individualistic, and too involved with controversial social issues to be allied with these refined writers. Boyesen's gentility was balanced by another counter. He was not hostile toward the popular belief in science and progress, as were members of the Genteel Tradition, and he was free of their cultural heritage. He was neither descended from America's oldest aristocratic line nor an inheritor of the vestiges of Calvinism.

The impulse of late nineteenth century letters in England and America was to seek as Matthew Arnold did for a substitute for lost religious faith. The Genteel Tradition turned backward, attempting to keep alive the spirit of transcendentalism and the reason of neo-Augustan humanism. A realist like Howells saw the futility of such backward looks, discrediting these refined attempts along with his dismissal of Romanticism. The truth plainly told, to Howells, would provide morally regenerative literature. Science obviously held some truth in it, and since scientific methods had not been rigorously applied to literature in America, who could say that a wedding of science and literature, by providing men with an unadulterated actuality, would not help redeem an age where people deluded themselves by false attachments to the past? For a Realist like James, obviously the subtleties of human psychology and the powers of human imagination offered some compensation for loss of faith. Boyesen, superficially, seems to be either like the authoritarian establishment of the Genteel Tradition seeking a past humanism or like the devotees of social Darwinism who see man progressing toward a day when science and religion are one. While such a contradiction seems irreconcilable, it is consistent with Boyesen's own peculiar Naturalistic neo-Augustanism. He never made a choice between spirit and matter, mind and body, and authority and the individual, but instead desired, in the mood of the Augustan golden mean, to keep his irreconcilable opposites in balance.

As Laurence M. Larson points out, it is likely that Boyesen's reaction to Romanticism was conservative—directed toward the Augustan past—rather than liberal—directed toward the avant garde Realistic future: "Perhaps he could accept the new beliefs in the sovereignty of genius and in the identification of poetry with philosophy; but the pallid mysticism of Novalis' and Schlegel's demand for complete freedom, even within the marriage relation, could have no attraction for a man who, though somewhat critical of social conditions, was by no means ready to dispute the essential rightness of the social structure."[3] Boyesen did not ultimately take sides in the struggle of individuals against institutions in America. "The conservative bias of the philistine (though not so outwardly attractive) is no less valuable as a factor in civilization than the iconoclastic zeal of the reformer."[4] Boyesen goes on to justify the exclusion of writers like Byron and Shelley from society because society must protect itself against the rebel. Statements such as these, out of context, identify Boyesen with stifling traditionalism. Yet Boyesen in his fiction not only celebrated fathers and representatives of authority, but also celebrated rebellious sons and individuals who obeyed their romantic instincts, the promptings of the heart.

Boyesen is being neither hypocritical nor indecisive when he fails to decide between opposites. The opposites of his golden mean can also be the struggling counters in the battle for survival of the fittest. Here was Boyesen's new religion, described ably by John Fiske, but represented imaginatively nowhere so well as by Boyesen. Irreconcilable opposites were at war both in the real and in his fictional world. But ultimately, the universe was progressing toward a goal defined by science but consistent with religion. As Henry Steele Commager notes, "Evolution outmoded rather than nullified the Enlightenment and Transcendentalism, for though its methods were profoundly different its conclusions were much the same."[5] Evolution combines Boyesen's Augustan predilections with his Romantic yearnings, for as Josiah Royce pointed out in his contemporary study, "The doctrine of evolution . . . is in heart and essence the child of the romantic movement."[6]

Thus, it does not seem essential to determine whether Boyesen was Realistic or Romantic or whether he was Augustan or Romantic. In an intellectually eclectic time, he managed to make his own synthesis, not a striking one for its quality of thought, but impressive when demonstrated in fiction.

Boyesen's writing represents an attempt to reconcile the discordant elements of his age. It was meant to have a moral and perhaps even a religious value. It came close to American popular culture because, unlike Howells and James, Boyesen seemed to be trying to keep alive the American dream of reconciling nature with progress, spiritual goals with material goals, and belief in freedom with the desire for order. While Mark Twain demonstrated that "progress" was sham and James showed men scrambling too late to develop spirits after lives committed to matter, and while most political writings showed the individual being crushed, Boyesen optimistically assumed that the direction of evolution would carry us beyond these problems. The problems, in fact, proved that the healthy struggle continued. While men in other novels were foolish over the girl, Boyesen had heroes who held out for a woman who offered redemption as one of her charms. Yet marriage with the right girl did not assure bliss everlasting. Life was a struggle, and ironically, good men got crushed. But other good men are rewarded. Perhaps if the larger pattern could be seen as the direction of evolutionary progress, we would not despair.

II *Boyesen's Place in Literary History*

Literary fame during one's life often has little to do with lasting literary fame. Boyesen had reason to believe that he had joined the immortals of literature. Not only had he been a staunch advocate of the newest theories of literature, an importer of European culture, but he had made his synthesis with tradition. His very titles, *The Daughter of the Philistines, The Golden Calf, The Mammon of Unrighteousness,* all biblical, indicate that he felt that his novels dealt with eternal problems—the struggle of good and evil, the individual against the masses, the spiritual against the material. Had not Sophocles done the same? Yet despite Boyesen's eternal themes, the later twentieth century reader is bound to see his novels as quaint and to look upon his treatment of moral issues as shallow and perhaps—to use the current most damning epithet—irrelevant.

Even those who have read Boyesen thoroughly seem not to recommend that we do likewise. Both Clarence Glasrud's biography, *Hjalmar Hjorth Boyesen,* and Marc Ratner's unpublished dissertation, "Hjalmar Hjorth Boyesen: Critic of Literature and Society,"[7] accept Boyesen's failure as a writer of fiction. Mr. Glasrud's useful biography was written to document the importance of the Norwegian-American "as a pioneer realist and liaison man between European and American literature."[8] Ratner's dissertation involves intellectual history and the role Darwinism played in Boyesen's thought and writing. To these scholars, neither Boyesen the pioneer realist nor Boyesen the social Darwinist was original in art or thought. He is interesting to them because his accomplishment was remarkable for an immigrant or because he represents well an intellectual milieu.

In addition to these full-length studies of Boyesen, such famous critics as Alfred Kazin, Granville Hicks, and Vernon L. Parrington have read Boyesen and given him attention, usually not flattering, in their writings. Kazin calls Boyesen's novels

failures "not only because Boyesen was compromised by 'pru-
dence,' but largely because, like so many of his daring contemporaries, he was not happy in realism." Boyesen "did his best work
in his romantic children's stories of Norwegian life."[9] For Hicks
Boyesen's failure rested in his attempt to use an ethical theory
as the best clue to understanding America. In his analysis of
nineteenth century America, Boyesen had "understood part of
the change that was going on, but not enough to make his characters fully representative. Earnestness and indignation had done
what they could, but something more was needed."[10] Parrington
regards Boyesen as a writer of primarily historical interest who
has fallen from favor because of his mistaken attempt to wed
individualistic psychological Realism and sociological fiction.[11]
In this failure, however, Parrington, along with others, sees Boyesen as a precursor of Naturalism in America.

    These critics have at least read Boyesen, and significantly, they
do not identify him with Howells. The specter of Howells in
every case, however, hangs over their judgment. To Kazin, Boyesen's "tepid soul"[12] causes him to fail to write realistically.
Unlike Howells, he did not experience "the transformation of
American life after the Civil War almost as a personal disaster."[13]
Boyesen's theoretical side was Tennysonian, "and not half so
challenging as George Eliot." To Kazin, apparently Boyesen's
theories are merely intrusions into his fictional world, and what
is left is merely his "vigor of conscience."[14] With wooden characterization and a bad ear for dialogue, Boyesen "lacked a
necessary flair for the novel."[15] To Hicks also, it is Boyesen's
capacity for theorizing which causes him to fail at realistic depiction of characters. Only Parrington seems to understand what
Boyesen intended in his ethical and sociological approach to
characterization. To Parrington, however, Boyesen is too psychological for a writer who intended to be sociological. He would
never grant that Boyesen, like Howells, was mediating "between
men and an immoral society."[16]

    In part, the problem of Boyesen's failure to earn a permanent
place in literary history is a consequence of his lacking "a necessary flair for the novel." Yet there are moments, indeed large
sections of his work, in which his irony is superb, his realistic
descriptions engaging, and the credibility of his characteriza-

tions considerable. If he lacked entirely that flair, a study such as this would not be worth undertaking.

Boyesen's failure to gain immortality stems from two factors. One is that while he had talent, he had little creativity. In other words, despite his radical theorizing, Boyesen as a practitioner of the novel form in an age when the forms of fiction were in transition was largely a quite conventional writer. While he chose Realistic material, he often let his Augustan tendency to relate the part to the whole overwhelm the particular. What is astonishing about Howells, on the other hand, is that he often offered complete detailed pictures without so much as hinting what they meant; unadulterated reality was enough. In addition, Boyesen was not really content to deal with the ordinary characters of Realistic fiction. His middle class heroes and heroines had to be like knights or princesses. His most important characters had to have a light to their countenances which transformed banalities. Moreover, in an age when James was questioning how much the vantage point of fiction affected the type of reality portrayed, Boyesen was doing little experimentation with point of view. His seemingly omniscient narrators imply that there are no epistemological problems.

Second, one must fault Boyesen's treatment of experience. Contrary to his belief in his own worldliness, and paradoxically for a man of two cultures, it was limited. Limited experience may not harm the writing of a man interested in intensiveness—for example, the psychological probings of James or the analysis of subtle problems of a relationship in Howells—but the mood of Boyesen's writing is expansive, not intensive. Yet in his expansiveness, one senses that Boyesen really only knew one manner of life well. He is most believable in attacking society matriarchs. His pictures of opulent life are effectively specific. Boyesen, the judge's grandson, the society dame's husband, the summer resident of Southhampton, knew the affluent life of two countries, and surprisingly, they are not much different from each other. His picture of immigrant life and political life, subject matter which, he felt, distinguished him among writers, seems artificial, not really specific enough. Perhaps as an academic person writing novels, he was too far removed from the turmoil of American life to handle it effectively. While exceptions to the limitations that I have specified exist—especially *The Mammon of Unrighteousness* and *The Golden Calf*—even these novels are stilted when they wander away from gracious upper middle class Victorian life.

Yet despite his failings, Boyesen is an important literary figure. His place in literary history is that of the professional man of letters, a phenomenon that has since declined and nearly disappeared. Boyesen, whose criticism was journalistic rather than intensive, may have contributed to the demise of the class of men he represented. Moreover, his life as an academic, instead of enhancing his experience and enriching his work, removed him from the life of the streets which provided Crane with substance and from the life of thoughtful, nonpurposive leisure which James lived. Boyesen, however, helped give cohesiveness to the world of letters at a time when the breakup of the American literary scene into its current fragmentary state was imminent. American literature throughout has been characterized by loners, private poets, alienated, nearly mad men, and independent innovators. Thoreau, Emerson, and others two generations before Boyesen formed the closest thing America had had to a self-conscious literary movement. Yet the intense individualism of American Romanticism was bound to make their alliance fragile. In Boyesen's generation, a feeling of a movement again developed. In a culture such as this, which distrusts literature for both moral and pragmatic reasons, Boyesen's circle (which by rights should be called Howells' circle) demonstrated that literature had a place that was not merely decorative in the most Philistine of ages. The man of letters at Boyesen's time, whose frenzied busyness resembled that of the industrialist, held out the hope that the banalities of American life could be redeemed through literature. Without the public relations work of Boyesen (he spoke with the authority of the academic and the genteel), Howells may not have found the literary world so congenial. Boyesen helped to create an atmosphere which made possible the growth of a movement. Without men such as he, America might well have had, during this period of great material growth, no time for letters.

Besides his function as a man of letters, it is difficult to isolate Boyesen's influence. Certainly both in his example and in the

Naturalistic writings from Europe which he introduced to American readers, Boyesen helped to create the climate for Naturalism in the United States. He was too comfortable, genteel, and prosperous, however, to feel the Naturalists' anger about the conditions of the country, the world, or the cosmos. His writings, therefore, had little direct influence. But possibly in an instance like this, a man's contribution should be measured in terms of an indirect influence. Boyesen's blending of the aspirations and ideals of popular culture with the most avant garde literary theory makes him resemble certain twentieth century writers more than he resembles his contemporaries. Certainly Hemingway and Fitzgerald earlier in this century and Updike and Pynchon currently all represent a kind of literary Realism in which there is present, nevertheless, a mysterious sense of possibility about the material world which is being described. This sense of mystery can be treated with great literary sophistication while still reflecting the most basic of American dreams—that somehow in this culture, the material can be made ideal. In fact, Boyesen's themes and methods seem more prevalent today than the detached, unromantic Realism of Howells. If American writing is characterized currently by a new Romanticism, Boyesen may have prepared the ground for this development.

Notes and References

Preface

1. Edmund Wilson, *Patriotic Gore* (New York: Oxford University Press, 1962), p. 707.
2. William Dean Howells, *A Hazard of New Fortunes* (New York: Bantam Books, 1960), p. 16.

Chapter One

1. Laurence M. Larson, *The Changing West and Other Essays* (Northfield, Minn.: Norwegian-American Historical Association, 1937), lists in a footnote, pp. 114–15, the pallbearers as their names appeared in *The Columbia University Bulletin*, no. 12, p. 45. This list included Columbia University President Seth Low, Professors J. H. van Amringe, Nicholas Murray Butler, Munroe Smith, Brander Matthews, and W. H. Carpenter, and other well-known names, including William Dean Howells, E. C. Stedman, Richard Watson Gilder, Hamilton W. Mabie, Carl Schurz, Charles S. Fairchild, Salem H. Wales, John DeWitt Warner, John Brisbane Walker, and Dr. Gallard Thomas.
2. "Writing My First Book," *Philadelphia Inquirer*, October 1, 1893, p. 10.
3. Vernon L. Parrington, *Main Currents in American Thought*, III (New York: Harcourt and Brace, 1939), p. 182.
4. Alfred Kazin, *On Native Ground* (New York: Reynal and Hitchcock, 1942), p. 10.
5. Most of the major facts of Boyesen's life can be found in Larson and in Clarence Glasrud, *Hjalmar Hjorth Boyesen* (Northfield, Minn.: Norwegian-American Historical Association, 1963). I have supplemented from other sources and have added some interpretations of facts where it seemed wanting.
6. "The Story of an Outcast," in *Tales from Two Hemispheres* (Boston: J.R. Osgood, 1876), pp. 84–85.
7. "A Norse Emigrant," *Galaxy*, 15 (February 1873), p. 199.
8. The letters of Austa Boyesen, Boyesen's sister, to Laurence M. Larson are in the Larson Collection, University of Illinois Library, Urbana. This letter is also quoted in Larson, p. 82.

9. Glasrud, p. 6.

10. Ibid., p. 8.

11. "Norwegian Hospitality," *Lippincott's*, 8 (February, 1894), p. 267.

12. "Immigration," *National Perils and Opportunities: Evangelical Conference for the United States of America* (New York: Baker and Taylor, 1887), p. 73.

13. William Dean Howells, *Literary Friends and Acquaintance* (New York: Harper and Brothers, 1900), p. 267.

14. "Writing My First Book," p. 10.

15. Ibid.

16. Howells, *Literary Friends and Acquaintance*, p. 256.

17. W. D. Howells wrote Boyesen frequently during this period, sympathizing and encouraging his writing. These letters are among the Boyesen Papers, Columbia University Library.

18. "Writing My First Book," p. 10.

19. Ibid.

20. "A Visit to Tourguenieff," *Galaxy*, 17 (April 1874), 457.

21. Arlin Turner, "A Novelist Discovers a Novelist," *Western Humanities Review*, 5 (Autumn 1951), p. 354. The letter quoted is January 20, 1878.

22. Ibid., p. 355.

23. Cable to Boyesen, January 3, 1878; Turner, p. 351.

24. Boyesen to Cable, January 20, 1878; Turner, p. 353.

25. Ibid., pp. 353–54.

26. Boyesen dedicated *Ilka on the Hill Top* to his wife's doctor, Egbert Guernsey, evidently in partial repayment for his care of Mrs. Boyesen.

27. *Author*, 2 (March 15, 1890), p. 36.

28. Howells, *Literary Friends and Acquaintance*, p. 260.

29. William H. Carpenter, "In Memorium," *Columbia University Bulletin*, 12 (December 1895), pp. 48–49.

30. "Writing My First Book," p. 10.

Chapter Two

1. Nathaniel Hawthorne, *The Scarlet Letter*, ed. Harry Levin (New York: Houghton Mifflin, 1960), p. 38.

2. Samuel Taylor Coleridge, *Biographia Literaria*, ed. J. Shawcross (London: Clarendon, 1907), II, p. 3.

3. *Gunnar* (Boston: J. R. Osgood, 1874), p. 1, was serialized in *Atlantic*, 32 (July-December 1873). Further references are cited in the text.

4. Boyesen quotes Turgenev's criticism of his first chapter in a letter to John Fiske, November 30, 1873. The letters to Fiske are in the Fiske Collection, Cornell University Library, Ithaca, New York.

5. James Joyce, *A Portrait of the Artist as a Young Man* (New York: Viking, 1962), p. 65.

6. "The Mountain's Face," in *Queen Titania* (New York: Scribner's, 1881), p. 183.

7. "Truls, the Nameless," in *Tales from Two Hemispheres*, p. 221, first appeared in *Scribner's*, 9 (April 1875), 731–36. Further references are cited in the text.

8. Even in late stories, for example the novella "A Harvest of Tares," *Godey's*, 126 (May 1893), 527–616, Boyesen uses America as a symbol of imaginative freedom. The Norwegian heroine rejects marriage with a Norwegian clergyman in order to flee to America to marry an artist. This story, however, is at such variance with other work Boyesen did late in his career that it seems merely a reversion, a sentimental return to his lost Romanticism.

9. Both stories are included in *Tales from Two Hemispheres*. "The Story of an Outcast" (pp. 83–128) appeared first in *Scribner's*, 9 (November 1874), 38–48, and "Asathor's Vengeance" (pp. 244–283) appeared first in *Atlantic*, 35 (March 1875), 345.

10. "Asathor's Vengeance," in *Tales from Two Hemispheres*, p. 263.

11. Ibid., p. 273.

12. Ibid.

13. "A Scientific Vagabond," in *Tales from Two Hemispheres*, pp. 178–220, first appeared in *Scribner's* 11 (December 1875), 229–39.

14. "A Good for Nothing," *Tales from Two Hemispheres*, p. 177, first appeared in *Scribner's*, 10 (July 1875), 361–72.

Chapter Three

1. Howells, *Literary Friends and Acquaintance*, pp. 257–60.

2. September 27, 1880, Boyesen Papers, Columbia University Library.

3. *Falconberg* (New York: Scribner's, 1879), p. 6, was serialized in *Scribner's*, 16–17 (August 1878–April 1879).

4. "A Norse Emigrant," p. 203.

5. *A Norseman's Pilgrimage* (New York: Sheldon and Company, 1875), p. 50. Further references are cited in the text.

6. "Hjalmar Hjorth Boyesen," *Library of the World's Best Literature*, V, ed. Charles D. Warner (New York: J. A. Hill, 1897), pp. 2273–74.

7. *A Norseman's Pilgrimage*, p. 195.

8. *Falconberg*, p. 24. Further references are cited in the text.

9. "Under the Glacier," in *Ilka on the Hill Top*, pp. 86–126 (New York: Scribner's, 1881). The story also appeared in *Scribner's*, 21 (December 1880), 234–45.

10. "A Perilous Incognito," in *Vagabond Tales*, pp. 234–84 (New York: D. Lothrop, 1889). The story first appeared in *Scribner's*, 2 (July–August 1887), 120–28; 222–28.

11. "A Perilous Incognito," *Vagabond Tales*, p. 282.

12. "A Child of the Age," in *Vagabond Tales*, pp. 34–97. The story first appeared in *Century*, 31 (December 1885), 177–92.

13. "The Man Who Lost His Name," in *Tales From Two Hemispheres*, pp. 9–82. The story appeared first in *Scribner's* 12 (November 1876), 808–26.

14. "A Knight of Danneborg," in *Ilka on the Hill Top*, pp. 127–29. The story first appeared in *Scribner's*, 19 (February 1880), 593–608.

15. "Liberty's Victim," in *Vagabond Tales*, pp. 183–233.

16. "Monk Tallenbach's Exile," in *Vagabond Tales*, pp. 98–141.

17. "A Dangerous Virtue," *Queen Titania*, pp. 188–89, first appeared in *Scribner's*, 21 (March 1881), 745–59. Further references are cited in the text.

18. "A Disastrous Partnership," in *Vagabond Tales*, pp. 142–82.

19. Ibid., p. 180.

20. "Song of Myself," 3, *Leaves of Grass*, 1855.

Chapter Four

1. Wilson, p. 708.

2. Noel Annan, *New York Review of Books*, February 12, 1970, p. 11.

3. *Literary History of the United States*, ed. Robert Spiller et al. (New York: Macmillan, 1963), p. 15.

4. William Wasserstrom, *Heiress of All the Ages* (Minneapolis: University of Minnesota Press, 1959), p. 126.

5. John Milton, *Paradise Lost*, IV (1667), l. 339.

6. Wasserstrom, p. vii.

7. Delia Saunders serves as a foil for the heroine, Constance Douglas, in *The Light of Her Countenance* (New York: D. Appleton, 1889).

8. *The Light of Her Countenance*, p. 36.

9. James Bryce, *The American Commonwealth*, 3rd ed. (New York: Macmillan, 1940), p. 681.

10. Wasserstrom, p. 18.

11. Ibid., p. 69.

12. *Literary and Social Silhouettes* (New York: Harper Bros., 1894), p. 2. Further references are cited in the text.

13. In this scene in *A Norseman's Pilgrimage*, Miss Copely has been arguing a characteristically American position, that America, despite its short history, is not lacking in the material necessary for great art. When she claims that any American home twenty years old has seen as much human tragedy and romance as a European home centuries old, Varberg says, "Yes, if you would call a drunken shoemaker who ruins his family a romantic character" (77).

Ruth then, in American Puritan fashion, forgets the logical direction of the argument by inserting a defense of American temperance against European intemperate depravity.

14. "The Man Who Lost His Name," p. 49.

15. "The Evolution of the Heroine," *Lippincott's*, 14 (September 1894), p. 426.

16. Ibid., p. 427.

17. Wasserstrom, p. ix.

18. Wasserstrom, p. 127.

19. *Falconberg*, p. 171.

20. *The Light of Her Countenance*, p. 195.

21. Ibid., p. 125.

22. "The Man Who Lost His Name," p. 39.

23. Ibid., p. 33 (emphasis added).

24. "How Mr. Storm Met His Destiny," in *Ilka on the Hill Top*, pp. 206–40, appeared first in *Scribner's*, 13 (February 1877), 547–59.

25. *The Light of Her Countenance*, p. 277. Further references are cited in the text.

26. "The Horns of a Dilemma," in *Continent*, 4 (September 26, 1883), 386–404. Further references are cited in the text.

27. "Swart Among the Buckeyes," in *Scribner's*, 14 (August 1877), pp. 547–79.

28. "Queen Titania," *Queen Titania* (New York: Scribner's, 1881), pp. 1–37.

29. Wasserstrom, p. 74.

30. Ibid., p. 76.

31. "The Story of a Blue Vein," *Cosmopolitan*, 1 (March 1886), pp. 3–16.

32. Ibid., p. 6.

33. Ibid., p. 5.

34. "Annunciata," in *Ilka on the Hill Top*, pp. 41–85, first appeared in *Scribner's*, 18 (October 1879), 911–23. "Anastasia," *Scribners*, 25 (April 1883), 839–52.

35. "Charity," in *Vagabond Tales,* pp. 285–332, first appeared in *Scribner's,* 4 (October 1888), 490–506.
36. *The Daughter of the Philistines* (Boston: Robert Bros., 1883), p. 7. The story begins quite similarly in thought and tone to Jane Austen's *Pride and Prejudice.* Further references are cited in the text.
37. "A Problematic Character," *Century,* 28 (August-October 1884), 608–9; 745–60; 893–902.
38. Ibid., p. 608.
39. Ibid., p. 755.
40. "The New Womanhood," *Lippincott's,* 56 (July 1895), pp. 126–30.
41. *Literary and Social Silhouettes,* pp. 48–49.

Chapter Five

1. Howells, *Literary Friends and Acquaintance,* p. 265.
2. *Criticism and Fiction,* ed. Clara and Rudolf Kirk (New York: New York University Press, 1959), p. 15.
3. Ibid.
4. *Literary and Social Silhouettes,* pp. 22–23.
5. See "A Defense of the Eighth Commandment," *Cosmopolitan,* 4 (February 1888), 485-89.
6. Howells, *Criticism and Fiction,* p. 282.
7. *Literary and Social Silhouettes,* p. 51.
8. Howells, *Criticism and Fiction,* p. 62.
9. Ibid., p. 38.
10. *Literary and Social Silhouettes,* p. 71.
11. *Essays on Scandinavian Literature* (New York: Scribner's, 1895), p. 116.
12. Ibid., p. 99.
13. *Essays on German Literature* (New York: Scribner's, 1892), p. 3.
14. Ibid.
15. See Boyesen's "On Zola's Experimental Novel," *Cosmopolitan,* 17 (August 1894), p. 506; his essay on Brandes in *Essays on Scandinavian Literature,* pp. 205ff; his "Social Problems in Norwegian Novels," *Critic,* 7 (September 19, 1885), pp. 133–34; and his *A Commentary on the Writings of Henrik Ibsen* (London: W. Heineman, 1894).
16. *Essays on Scandinavian Literature,* p. 122.
17. *Goethe and Schiller* (New York: Scribner's, 1879), p. 285.
18. *Essays on Scandinavian Literature,* p. 205.
19. "Social Problems in Norwegian Novels," pp. 133–34.

20. Howells, *Literary Friends and Acquaintance*, p. 260.
21. *Literary and Social Silhouettes*, p. 46.
22. Howells, *Criticism and Fiction*, p. 67.
23. Ibid., p. 13.
24. *Literary and Social Silhouettes*, pp. 184–85.
25. *Essays on Scandinavian Literature*, p. 98.
26. Howells, *Criticism and Fiction*, pp. 337–39.
27. "On Zola's Experimental Novel," p. 506.
28. Howells, *Criticism and Fiction*, p. 162 (emphasis added).
29. *Essays on Scandinavian Literature*, p. 99.

Chapter Six

1. Henry Adams, "Buddah and Brahma," *Yale Review*, 5 (1915), p. 88.
2. Henry Adams, *Democracy* (New York: Farrar, Strauss and Young, 1952).
3. "The Hope of Nations," *Independent*, 40 (January 19, 1888), pp. 66–67. Further references are cited in the text.
4. "Mars and Apollo," *Chautauquan*, 48 (July 1888), p. 585.
5. "Victims of Progress," *Independent*, 40 (May 17, 1888), p. 610. Further references are cited in text.
6. "A New World Fable: The World's Fair," *Cosmopolitan*, 16 (December 1893), pp. 173–86. Further references are cited in the text.
7. "German Student Life," *Cosmopolitan*, 10 (January 1891), p. 368.
8. "The University of Rome," *Scribner's*, 18 (September 1879), p. 661.
9. "Where Should a College Be Located? In a City," *Chautaquan*, 13 (July 1891), pp. 467–68.
10. "German Student Life," p. 371.
11. "The University of Berlin," *Century*, 18 (June 1879), pp. 205–17.
12. "On the University of Chicago," *Cosmopolitan*, 14 (April 1893), pp. 665–73. "Cornell University," *Cosmopolitan*, 8 (November 1888), pp. 59–66.
13. "The Chautauquan Movement," *Cosmopolitan*, 19 (June 1895), p. 147.
14. "The Ethics of Robert Browning," *Independent*, 40 (December 13, 1888), pp. 1595–96.
15. "The Problem of Happiness," *Independent*, 40 (November 15, 1888), pp. 1457–58. Further references are cited in the text.
16. Alfred Lord Tennyson, *In Memoriam*, 14: ll. 5–6.

17. "The Ethics of Robert Browning," p. 1595. Further references are cited in the text.

18. "Juxtaposition of Races," *Cosmopolitan*, 15 (August 1893), p. 504.

19. "The Dangers of Unrestricted Immigration," *Forum*, 3 (July 1887), p. 535.

20. Ibid., p. 541.

21. "Village Life in Norway," *Chautauquan*, 18 (October 1893), p. 8.

22. "Juxtaposition of Races," p. 504.

23. "Philistinism," *Independent*, 140 (September 27, 1888), p. 1225.

24. Ibid., p. 1226.

25. "American Literary Criticism and Its Value," *Forum*, 15 (June 1893), p. 462.

26. "Mars and Apollo," p. 585.

27. "The French Academy," *Independent*, 37 (January 1, 1885), p. 6.

28. Ibid.

29. "On Ibsen's Poems," *Cosmopolitan*, 15 (May 1893), p. 98.

Chapter Seven

1. Turner, p. 346.

2. *The Mammon of Unrighteousness* (New York: U. S. Book Co., 1891), p. 5. Further references are cited in the text.

3. *The Golden Calf* (Meadville, Pa.: Flood and Vincent, 1892), p. 109. Further references are cited in the text.

4. Minna's unchallenged goodness, while attractive, has little power. In stories such as "A Candidate for Divorce," *Cosmopolitan*, 8 (March 1890), 582–626, and "A Platonic Affair," *Harper's*, 80 (February 1890), 347–62, Boyesen shows a woman and a man who are temperamentally unfit for survival in a materialistic world because of their naively idealistic education.

5. *Social Strugglers* (New York: Scribner's, 1893), p. 9.

Chapter Eight

1. Frederick I. Carpenter, *American Literature and the Dream* (New York: Philosophical Library, 1955), p. 89.

2. Ibid., pp. 58–59.

3. Larson, p. 100.

4. "A Prince of Critics," *Christian Union*, 43 (January 22, 1891), p. 106.

5. Henry Steele Commager, *The American Mind* (New Haven: Yale University Press, 1950), p. 87.

6. Josiah Royce, *The Spirit of Modern Philosophy* (Boston: Houghton Mifflin, 1892), p. 305.

7. New York University, 1959.

8. Glasrud, p. vii.

9. Kazin, p. 27.

10. Granville Hicks, *The Great Tradition* (New York: Macmillan, 1933), p. 158.

11. Parrington, p. 182.

12. Kazin, p. 27.

13. Ibid., p. 38.

14. Ibid., p. 28.

15. Ibid.

16. Ibid., p. 40.

Selected Bibliography

PRIMARY SOURCES

1. Novels (in chronological order)

Gunnar. Boston: J. R. Osgood, 1874.
A Norseman's Pilgrimage. New York: Shelden and Company, 1875.
Falconberg. New York: Scribner's, 1879.
The Daughter of the Philistines. Boston: Robert Bros., 1883.
The Light of Her Countenance. New York: D. Appleton, 1889.
The Mammon of Unrighteousness. New York: U. S. Book Co., 1891.
The Golden Calf. Meadville, Pa.: Flood and Vincent, 1892.
Social Strugglers. New York: Scribner's, 1893.

2. Story Collections (in chronological order)

Tales from Two Hemispheres. Boston: J. R. Osgood, 1876.
Queen Titania. New York: Scribner's, 1881.
Ilka on the Hilltop. New York: Scribner's, 1881.
The Modern Vikings. New York: Scribner's, 1887.
Vagabond Tales. New York: D. Lothrop, 1889.
Against Heavy Odds. New York: Scribner's, 1890.
A Fearless Trio. New York: Scribner's, 1890.
Norseland Tales. New York: Scribner's, 1891.

3. Book Length Criticism, Academic Materials, and Others

Goethe and Schiller. New York: Scribner's, 1879.
Idylls of Norway and Other Poems. New York: Scribner's, 1882.
Alpine Roses (play). New York: Scribner's, 1884.
The Story of Norway. New York: G. Putnam's Sons, 1886.
How to Choose a School. New York: Teachers College Education
    Leaflet 65, 1890.
Essays on German Literature. New York: Scribner's, 1892.
Boyhood in Norway. New York: Scribner's, 1892.
A Commentary on the Writings of Henrik Ibsen. London: W. Heine-
    man, 1894.

174

Literary and Social Silhouettes. New York: Harper Bros., 1894.
Essays on Scandinavian Literature. New York: Scribner's, 1895.

4. Selected Short Stories and Novellas (in chronological order)

"A Norse Emigrant." *Galaxy,* 15 (February 1873), 199.
"The Story of An Outcast." *Scribner's,* 9 (November 1874), 36–48.
"Asathor's Vengeance." *Atlantic,* 35 (March 1875), 345.
"Truls, the Nameless." *Scribner's,* 9 (April 1875), 731–36.
"A Good for Nothing." *Scribner's,* 10 (July 1875), 361–72.
"A Scientific Vagabond." *Scribner's,* 11 (December 1875), 229–39.
"The Man Who Lost His Name." *Scribner's,* 12 (November 1876), 808–26.
"How Mr. Storm Met His Destiny." *Scribner's,* 13 (February 1877), 547–59.
"Swart Among the Buckeyes." *Scribner's,* 14 (August 1877), 547–57.
"Annunciata." *Scribner's,* 18 (October 1879), 911–23.
"A Knight of Danneborg." *Scribner's,* 19 (February 1880), 593–608.
"Under the Glacier." *Scribner's,* 21 (December 1880), 234–45.
"A Dangerous Virtue." *Scribner's,* 21 (March 1881), 745–59.
"A Highly Respectable Family." *Harper's,* 64 (March 1882), 571–76.
"Anastasia." *Scribner's,* 25 (April 1883), 839–52.
"The Horns of a Dilemma." *Continent,* 4 (September 26, 1883), 386–404.
"A Problematic Character." *Century,* 28 (August-October 1884), 608–19; 745–60; 893–902.
"A Daring Fiction." *New York Commercial Advertiser,* November 15, 1884, Supplement.
"Mr. Block's One Glorious Night." *Harper's,* 29 (March 7, 1885), 154.
"A Child of the Age." *Century,* 31 (December 1885), 177–92.
"The Story of a Blue Vein." *Cosmopolitan,* 1 (March 1886), 3–16.
"Crooked John." *Century,* 34 (July 1887), 405–12.
"A Perilous Incognito." *Scribner's,* 2 (July-August 1887), 120–28; 222–28.
"Charity." *Scribner's,* 4 (October 1888), 490–506.
"The Two Mollies: A City Sketch." *Scribner's,* 6 (July 1889), 116–20.
"A Platonic Affair." *Harper's,* 80 (February 1890), 347–62.
"A Candidate for Divorce." *Cosmopolitan,* 8 (March 1890), 582–626.
"A Norse Atlantis." *Cosmopolitan,* 10 (November 1890), 48–68.
"Elixir of Pain." *Cosmopolitan,* 11 (May-July 1891), 62–87; 192–218; 347–67.
"A Harvest of Tares." *Godey's,* 126 (May 1893), 527–616.

"In Collusion with Fate." *Scribner's*, 20 (July 1896), 73–88.

5. Selected Poems (in chronological order)

"A Norse Stev." *Atlantic*, 29 (February 1872), 210.
"Thoralf and Synnev." *Atlantic*, 30 (October 1872), 403.
"The Bridge of Torrisdell." *Atlantic*, 31 (February 1873), 159.
"Norway." *Galaxy*, 15 (February 1873) 16.
"St. Olaf's Fountain." *Atlantic*, 31 (April 1873), 418.
"Four Sonnets." *Scribner's*, 25 (March 1878), 661–62.
"Evolution." *Atlantic*, 41 (May 1878), 565–67.
"Two Sonnets." *Lippincott's*, 28 (November 1881), 507.
"The Poet's Vocation." *Chautauquan*, 9 (January 1889), 222.
"To James R. Lowell on His Seventieth Birthday." *Critic*, 14 (February 23, 1889), 94.
"The Fisher Maiden's Song." *Century*, 51 (February 1896), 569.

6. Selected Essays and Reviews (in chronological order)

"Bjornson's Dramas." *North American Review*, 116 (January 1873), 109–38.
"A Visit to Tourgenieff." *Galaxy*, 17 (April 1874), 456–66.
"Social Aspects of the German Romantic School." *Atlantic*, 36 (July 1875), 49–57.
"Literary Aspects of the Romantic School." *Atlantic*, 37 (May 1876), 607–16.
"Tourgenieff." *Scribner's*, 14 (June 1877), 200–207.
"Reminiscences of Bayard Taylor." *Lippincott's*, 24 (August 1879), 209–16.
"The University of Berlin." *Century*, 18 (June 1879), 205–17.
"The University of Rome." *Scribner's*, 18 (September 1879), 654–67.
"Two Visits to Victor Hugo." *Scribner's*, 19 (December 1879), 184–93.
"Bjornstjerne Bjornson." *Scribner's*, 20 (July 1880), 336–45.
"G. W. Cable's *The Grandissimes*." *Scribner's*, 21 (November 1880), 159–61.
"Bjornson in the United States." *The Critic*, 1 (March 12, 1881), 58.
"Tourgenieff and the Nihilists." *Critic*, 1 (March 26, 1881), 81–82.
"Tourgenieff." *Critic*, 3 (September 22, 1883), 376–77.
"Reminiscences of Turgeniev." *Harper's*, 27 (September 29, 1883), 615.
"Cash Down or Percentage." *Critic*, 4 (February 9, 1884), 62.

"The Modern German Novel." *Princeton Review* (new series), 60 (March 1884), 154–68.

"The Dangers of Immigration." *Independent*, 36 (October 2, 1884), 1413–14.

"Hans Christian Andersen." *Dial*, 5 (November 1884), 159-62.

"The French Academy." *Independent*, 37 (January 1, 1885), 5–6.

"Social Problems in Norwegian Novels," *Critic*, 7 (September 19, 1885), 133–34.

'Author's Statements on International Copyright in 'Open Letters.' " *Scribner's*, 31 (February 1886), 628.

"Why We Have No Great Novelists." *Forum*, 2 (February 1887), 615–22.

"The Dangers of Unrestricted Immigration." *Forum*, 3 (July 1887), 532–42.

"The Hope of the Nations." *Independent*, 40 (January 19, 1888), 66–67.

"On the Writing of Novels." *Critic*, 12 (March 24, 1888), 136.

"Victims of Progress." *Independent*, 40 (May 17, 1888), 610.

"Mars and Apollo." *Chautauquan*, 8 (July 1888), 584–86.

"Philistinism." *Independent*, 40 (September 27, 1888), 1225–26.

"Cornell University." *Cosmopolitan*, 8 (November 1888), 59–66.

"The Romantic and Realistic Novel." *Chautauquan* (old series), 9 (November 1888), 96–98.

"The Problem of Happiness." *Independent*, 40 (November 15, 1888), 1457–58.

"The Ethics of Robert Browning." *Independent*, 40 (December 13, 1888), 1595–96.

"Two Reasons for Restricting Immigration." *Our Day*, 3 (February 1889), 127–38.

"The Hero in Fiction." *North American Review*, 148 (May 1889), 594–601.

"Henrik Ibsen." *Century*, 39 (March 1890), 794–96.

"German Student Life." *Cosmopolitan*, 10 (January 1891), 368–76.

"A Prince of Critics." *Christian Union*, 43 (January 22, 1891), 106.

"Where Should a College Be Located? In A City." *Chautauquan*, 13 (July 1891), 467–68.

"On Howells' Work." *Cosmopolitan*, 12 (February 1892), 502–503.

"The Unhappy Predicament of Emigrants." *Chautauquan*, 15 (August 1892), 607–10.

"On the University of Chicago." *Cosmopolitan*, 14 (April 1893), 665–73.

"On Ibsen's Poems." *Cosmopolitan*, 15 (May 1893), 91–99.

"American Literary Criticism and Its Value." *Forum,* 15 (June 1893), 459–66.
"Interview with Howells." *McClure's,* 1 (June 1893), 3–11.
"A German Novel." *Cosmopolitan,* 15 (July 1893), 378–79.
"Conversation with Bjornson." *Cosmopolitan,* 15 (August 1893), 413–22.
"Juxtaposition of Races." *Cosmopolitan,* 15 (August 1893), 504–505.
"Village Life in Norway." *Chautauquan,* 18 (October 1893), 1–8.
"Writing My First Book." *Philadelphia Inquirer,* October 1, 1893, p. 10.
"A New World Fable: The World's Fair." *Cosmopolitan,* 16 (December 1893), 173–86.
"On Zola's Experimental Novel." *Cosmopolitan,* 17 (August 1894), 506–07.
"The Evolution of the Heroine." *Lippincott's,* 54 (September 1894), 425–28.
"Great Realists and Empty Story-Tellers." *Forum,* 18 (February 1895), 724–31.
"The Chautauquan Movement." *Cosmopolitan,* 19 (June 1895), 147-58.
"The New Womanhood." *Lippincott's,* 56 (July 1895), 126–30.
"Woman's Position in Pagan Times." *Forum,* 20 (November 1895), 311–16.

7. Collections of Letters and Manuscripts

Boyesen Papers, Columbia University Library.
Cable Collection, Howard-Tilton Memorial Library, Tulane University, New Orleans.
Howells Collection, Houghton Library, Harvard University, Cambridge.

SECONDARY SOURCES

CARPENTER, FREDERIC I. *American Literature and the Dream.* New York: Philosophical Library, 1955. Discusses the relation of pragmatism, the Genteel Tradition, and other literary and philosophical currents to the American dream.
COMMAGER, HENRY STEELE. *The American Mind.* New Haven: Yale University Press, 1950. Intellectual history of the late nineteenth century.
COWLEY, MALCOLM. "Naturalism in American Literature." In *Evolutionary Thought in America,* ed. Stow Persons. New Haven:

Yale University Press, 1950. Traces the relation of evolution and Darwinism to literary Naturalism.

FISKE, JOHN H. *Outlines of Cosmic Philosophy*. New York: Houghton, Mifflin and Co., 1874. An important evolutionary cosmologist who influenced Boyesen.

GLASRUD, CLARENCE. "Boyesen and the Norwegian Immigration." *Norwegian-American Studies and Records*, 19 (1956), 15–45.

—————. *Hjalmar Hjorth Boyesen*. Northfield, Minn.: Norwegian-American Historical Association, 1963. The only biography. Concerns work as well as life.

HICKS, GRANVILLE. *The Great Tradition*. New York: Macmillan, 1933. Literary history which shows Boyesen's relation to other realists.

HOFSTADTER, RICHARD. *Social Darwinism in American Thought*. New York: G. Braziller, 1955. The intellectual historical overview of Boyesen's milieu.

HOIDAHL, AAGOT D. "Norwegian American Fiction, 1880–1928." *Norwegian-American Historical Association Studies and Records*, 5 (1930), 61–83. Places Boyesen among other Norwegian immigrant writers.

HOUGHTON, DONALD E. "Hjalmar Hjorth Boyesen: An Early Realist." Master's thesis, Columbia University, 1947. A brief general study.

KAZIN, ALFRED. *On Native Ground*. New York: Reynal and Hitchcock, 1942. Unsparingly spells out Boyesen's limitations. Indicates Boyesen is essentially unhappy working in Realism.

LARSON, LAURENCE M. "Hjalmar Hjorth Boyesen." In *The Changing West and Other Essays*. Northfield, Minn.: Norwegian-American Historical Association, 1937. The best source of biographical material on Boyesen. Also concerns other minor writers.

PAPASHVILY, HELEN WAITE. *All the Happy Endings*. New York: Harper, 1956. A good discussion of the characteristics of sentimental American literature of the nineteenth century.

PARRINGTON, VERNON L. *Main Currents in American Thought: The Beginnings of Critical Realism*. Vol. 3. New York: Harcourt and Brace, 1939. The best overall work on the Realistic period; places Boyesen's work in perspective.

RATNER, MARC. "Georg Brandes and Hjalmar Hjorth Boyesen." *Scandinavian Studies*, 33 (November 1961), 218–30.

—————. "Howells and Boyesen: Two Views of Realism." *New England Quarterly*, 35 (September 1962), 376–90.

—————. "The Iron Madonna: H. H. Boyesen's American Girl." *Jahrbuk fur Amerikastudien*, 9 (1964), pp. 166–72. Discussion of Boyesen's notion of American young women and their effect upon literature.

180 HJALMAR HJORTH BOYESEN

TURNER, ARLIN. "A Novelist Discovers a Novelist." *Western Humanities Review*, 5 (Autumn 1951), 343–73. Correspondence of Boyesen and George Washington Cable.

WALCUTT, CHARLES C. *American Literary Naturalism: A Divided Stream*. Minneapolis: University of Minnesota Press, 1956. Boyesen may belong in one of these currents of Naturalism.

WASSERSTROM, WILLIAM. *Heiress of all the Ages*. Minneapolis: University of Minnesota Press, 1959. A psychological discussion of the nineteenth century American heroine.

WHITE, GEORGE LEROY, JR. "H. H. Boyesen: A Note on Immigration." *American Literature*, 13 (January 1942), 363–71. Discusses Boyesen's ethnocentrism in his ideas about immigration.

————. *Scandinavian Themes in American Fiction*. Philadelphia: University of Pennsylvania, 1937. Mentions Boyesen as literary liaison with important Scandinavian writers.

Index

Adams, Henry, 116-17
Aldrich, Thomas Bailey, 156
Arnold, Matthew, 156
Anderson, Hans Christian, 23
Authors' Club, 28

Bernard, Claude, 18
Bjørnson, Bjørnsterne, 22, 23, 30, 76, 104, 110
Boyesen, Captain Sarolf (father), 19
Boyesen, Hjalmar Hjorth: Chautauqua speaker, 29-30; early career, 22-26; early years, 17-20; emigration, 20-22; life in New York City, 27-30; major phase, 30-31; marriage, 26-27; poetry, 29; teaching, 29

WORKS: NON-FICTION

"Ethics of Robert Browning, The," 121
Essays on German Literature, 30
Essays on Scandinavian Literature, 30
"Evolution of the Heroine, The," 103-104
Goethe and Schiller, 27
"Hope of Nations, The," 117-18
"Iron Madonna, The," 100-101
Literary and Social Silhouettes, 30, 77, 81-83
"Mars and Apollo," 118
"New World Fable, A," 118
"Problem of Happiness, The," 123
Story of Norway, The, 29
"Victims of Progress," 118-19

WORKS: FICTION

Alpine Roses, 29
"Anastasia," 96
"Annunciata," 96
"Asathor's Vengeance," 46, 47-48, 49
"Child of the Age, A," 68
"Charity," 96-97
"Dangerous Virtue, A," 28, 70-71
Daughter of the Philistines, A, 28, 83-84, 97-99, 108, 113, 114, 159
"Disastrous Partnership, A," 71, 72
Falconberg, 25, 50, 51, 59-66, 93, 99, 108
Golden Calf, A, 30, 31, 113, 114, 139-46, 148, 149, 152, 155, 159, 162
"Good for Nothing, A," 60-61
Gunnar, 22, 23, 32-43, 44, 45, 52, 53, 54, 57, 63, 76
"Horns of a Dilemma, The," 92-93
"How Mr. Storm Met his Destiny," 84
Ilka on the Hill Top, 28
"Ilka on the Hill Top," 66, 96
"Knight of Danneborg, A," 69
"Liberty's Victim," 69
Light of Her Countenance, The, 29, 31, 75, 80, 85-92, 99, 108-109
Mammon of Unrighteousness, The, 30, 31, 51, 113, 114, 128-39, 148, 149, 152, 159, 162
"Man Who Lost His Name, The," 68-69, 76, 78
"Monk Tellenbach's Exile," 69
"Mountain's Face, The," 43, 54
"Norse Emigrant, A," 66-67

181

Norseman's Pilgrimage, A, 20, 24,
52-59, 62, 66, 69, 76, 77, 84, 108
"Perilous Incognito, A" 67
"Problematic Character, A," 100
Queen Titania, 28
"Queen Titania," 94-95, 99
"Scientific Vagabond, A," 49
Social Strugglers, 31, 109, 113, 114,
124, *146-52*
"Story of a Blue Vein, A," 95-96
"Story of an Outcast, The," 46-47,
49-50, 67
"Swart Among the Buckeyes," 93,
96
Tales From Two Hemispheres, 25,
45
"Truls, the Nameless," 45-46, 47,
49, 52, 66, 71
Vagabond Tales, 28

Boyesen, Lillie Keene (wife), 26
Brandes, Georg, 17
Browning, Robert, 122-23, 125
Byron, Lord Gordon, 157

Cable, George Washington, 17, 25-
26, 31, 128
Chautauquas, 122, 125-26
Chicago World's Fair, 119-20
Child, Francis, 22
Coleridge, Samuel Taylor, 34, 108
Columbia College, 27, 28-29
Collins, Wilkie, 104
Commager, H.S., 158
Copyright law, 28, 103
Cornell University, 23, 24, 77, 121
Crane, Stephen, 154, 162

Darwin, Charles, 18
Darwinism, 72, 107, 115-16, 127,
130, 144-45, 152, 157, 159
Daudet, A., 104, 110
De Forest, J.W., 140
Dickens, Charles, 78
Dreiser, Theodore, 139, 146

Edwards, Jonathan, 72
Eggleston, Edward, 28, 30

Eliot, George, 78, 98, 122, 142
Emerson, R.W., 162
Emigration-Immigration,   30,   72,
123-25

Fitzgerald, F. Scott, 85, 163
Fiske, John, 158
Flaubert, Gustave, 99
Franklin, Benjamin, 72

Gaboriau, Emile, 104
Garland, Hamlin, 31
Genteel Tradition, 17, 156, 157
Gilder, Richard Watson, 24, 28
Glasrud, Clarence, 20, 159
Goethe, J.W. von, 108, 122

Hardy, Thomas, 35
Hawthorne, Nathaniel, 33-34, 43,
63, 108
Hicks, Granville, 159-60
Howells, William Dean, 17, 28, 32,
160, 162; *Criticism and Fiction,*
104; friendship with Boyesen,
22-23, 24; *A Hazard of New
Fortunes,* 116, 129, 150; *Literary
Friends and Acquaintance,* 51;
Rise of Silas Lapham, 150-51,
153-54; theory of realism, 102-
106, 109-14, 115, 156-58, 161
Holland, J.G., 24
Hopkins, Gerard Manley, 33

Ibsen, Henrik, 17, 24, 30, 104, 107,
112
Impressionism, 34
Industrialism, 118
International copyright law, 28

James, Henry, 22, 34, 52, 77, 87,
106, 109, 153-56, 158, 161
James, William, 153
Janson, Kristofer, 23, 30
Jewett, Sara Orne, 31
Joyce, James, 39, 42

Kazin, Alfred, 18, 159-60
Keats, John, 21, 38

Index

Keilland, Alexander, 107

Larson, Lawrence M. 157
Longfellow, Henry W., 22
Lowell, James Russel, 22

Marriage: proposal scenes, 83-84, 91; represented realistically, 28, 59, 129-30, 136-38, 149-50
Matthews, Brander, 28

Naturalism, naturalists, 17, 18, 30, 72, 101, 103, 104, 113, 131, 138-39, 146, 149, 160, 163
Nietzsche, Friedrich, 107
Norris, Frank, 103

Parrington, Vernon, 155, 159-60
Philistinism, 73, 126-27, 129
Pre-Raphaelitism, 33, 34, 40-41, 63
Progress, 118-20
Pynchon, Thomas, 163

Ratner, Mark, 159
Realism, 17, 18, 28, 29, 30, 31, 61-62, 78, 102-14, 115, 131-32, 151-52, 153; versus romanticism, 50, 56, 57, 58, 62-63, 64, 71, 72, 76, 77, 93, 101, 102-104, 125
Romanticism, 32-34, 44, 45, 50, 53, 72, 101, 102-104, 116, 131, 149, 163
Royce, Josiah, 158
Richardson, Samuel, 78, 104
Rolvaag, Ole, 65

Science and technology, 116, 118
Scott, Sir Walter, 20, 103, 104
Shakespeare, William, 21

Shelley, Percy Bysshe, 21, 122-23, 157
Social Darwinism: see Darwinism
Stedman, Edmund Clarence, 28, 133, 156
Swedenborgianism, 19, 21
Swineburne, August, 126

Taine, H.A., 18
Taylor, Bayard, 24
Tennyson, Alfred Lord, 123, 160
Thackery, William Makepeace, 18
Thoreau, H.D., 162
Tolstoi, Leo, 104
Turgenev, Ivan, 17, 22-23, 24, 28, 58, 108
Twain, Mark, 31, 103, 158

Universities, 120-21, 125-26
University of Chicago, 121
Updike, John, 163

Victorianism, 18, 74-75, 86; decorative art, 115-16

Wasserstrom, William, 74, 75, 81, 94-98
Wharton, Edith, 111
Whitman, Walt, 72
Wilson, Edmund, 72
Women: Audience for fiction, 100-101, 107; German vs. American, 81; heroines, types of, 78-82; idealized, 90-91, 92; nymphs and nuns, 82-84; represented realistically, 76-78; sexuality, 82; Victorian idea, 74-75
Wordsworth, William, 21, 31

Zola, Emile, 18, 104, 107, 111-12